P9-CFQ-637

COUNTDOWN TO ENCOUNTER

• • • • • • • • • • • • • • • • • •

Von Braun and the Astronauts

JOHN M. SCOTT

Our Sunday Visitor, Inc.
Huntington, Indiana 46750

Copyright© 1979 Our Sunday Visitor, Inc.

ISBN: 0-87973-630-5

Library of Congress Catalog Card Number: 79-84534

Cover Design by James E. McIlrath

Published, printed, and bound in the United States of America

630

DEDICATED TO THE MEMORY OF MY INSPIRING FRIEND
DR. WERNHER VON BRAUN,
WHOSE SPIRIT OF FAITH AND PRAYER
RAN THROUGH THE APOLLO PROJECT
LIKE A THREAD OF PURE GOLD IN A TAPESTRY

ACKNOWLEDGMENTS

Scriptural quotations in this work are taken primarily from *The New American Bible,* copyright© 1970 by the Confraternity of Christian Doctrine, Washington, D.C. Other Bible quotations are drawn from the Douay version of the Bible and from *The Jerusalem Bible,* originally published by Les Editions du Cerf, Paris, with English translation copyright© 1966, 1967, and 1968 by Darton, Longman & Todd, Ltd., London, and Doubleday & Company, Inc., New York.

The author and the publisher are grateful to the *New Catholic World* for permission to use poetry found on pages 36-37, and to Loyola University Press for permission to quote passages found on pages 58, 128-129, 135, 138, and 140-141.

If any protected materials have been inadvertently used without permission, we apologize and request notification from the copyright holder.

CONTENTS

Wernher von Braun: a man of vision, a man of faith. (Photo by Fabian Bachrach, New York)

INTRODUCTION

You are holding in your hands a unique book — a book that lets you discover for yourself the most inspiring fact of our space age.

In this book I'm sharing with you the one thing that impressed me most about our entire space program, from Dr. Wernher von Braun to the last astronauts to walk on the surface of the moon.

The inspiring fact is this: By and large our men of the space age have been men of faith and prayer. Our space program has been marked with a spirit of religion and confidence in God.

Many people are amazed when I inform them of some of the accounts which you will find in the pages of this book. And so, I thought it best, therefore, to gather into one volume many of the deeds and words of the men who brought this nation into the space age. I am sure that you will find these glimpses into the lives of our spacemen both thrilling and inspiring.

There is still another reason for writing this book. Dr. Wernher von Braun is dead. Project Apollo that landed our men on the moon is over. This first chapter in our space history is closed. In all likelihood, men will never again walk on the surface of the moon during our lifetime. Hence, it is high time that these events be captured in print.

Some of the facts mentioned in this book have appeared previously in some of my publications, but this is the first and only book to take the major events in our space history and combine them into one unit to show that faith and prayer were the dominant themes.

This book will show that the spirit of faith and prayer that dominated the life of von Braun ran through the entire Apollo project like a thread of pure gold in a tapestry.

While some of my previous publications mentioned individual astronauts, here you will find them in historical sequence and with much more detail.

In addition, this book shows how the Declaration of Faith of our modern-day spacemen is linked to the Declaration of Independence. Here is the inspiring account of America's dependence on God from our Founding Fathers to the astronauts.

The final chapter of this book deals with one of the greatest spinoffs of our space age — the awakening of our sense of wonder and awe, a modern-day gift of the Holy Spirit.

THE MAN WHO PUT US ON THE MOON

The walls of the Launch-Control Center rattled and shook like a snare drum. As flakes of plaster dust from the ceiling fell around him and technicians wildly cheered, Wernher von Braun breathed, "Go, baby, go."

It was Thursday, November 9, 1967, on Cape Kennedy's Launchpad 39A. America's mighty *Saturn 5*, taller than the Statue of Liberty, came to life as brilliant tongues of fire spewed out the flame buckets.

Generating seven and a half million pounds of thrust, the *Saturn 5* produced one of the loudest sounds ever heard by man, so loud, indeed, that the pressure waves were surpassed only by atmospheric nuclear blasts and two natural events — the Krakatoa volcano eruption of 1883 and the fall of the great Siberian meteorite in 1908.

The thundering *Saturn 5* rocket rose into the sky like an exclamation point with a fiery tail. It marked the climax of one era and stood up to shout the beginning of another. It announced to the world that the Apollo program was alive and leaping into the zenith.

Dr. Wernher von Braun, who coddled the *Saturn 5* from idea to steel in seven years of work, said of this moment, "It is undoubtedly the greatest moment of my life."

His "bird," the biggest thing ever to fly, climbed to a 117-mile orbit with a world-record satellite of 140 tons. From there the *Apollo* went out a lonely 11,386 miles and sizzled home into a rainy Pacific in a tough test of its heat shield.

From dream countdown to on-the-button lift-off to splashdown, the triumphant first outing of the three-stage, thirty-six-story *Saturn* booster and *Apollo's* dive back into the atmosphere at twenty-five thousand miles per hour was a "textbook" performance.

Newspapers heralded the flight of von Braun's bird as making November 9 a "grand day in space for the United States." Said President Johnson: "We can launch and bring back safely to earth the spaceship that will take men to the moon."

Much of America's progress in the space race has been due to the work of Dr. Wernher von Braun, our topmost rocket expert. It was Dr. von Braun himself who designed the Jupiter-C rocket, which lifted the first American earth satellite — *Explorer 1* — into orbit. This achievement, as he predicted at the time, "was only the beginning of our long-range program to conquer outer space."

Today Dr. von Braun is known as "the Father of the *Saturn*." He has become a legendary figure of modern rocketry. He was head of the billion-dollar George C. Marshall Space Flight Center at Huntsville, Alabama. He directed the teams which put America's first satellite into orbit and developed the world's largest rocket, which put our teams of Apollo astronauts on the moon.

Von Braun made it possible for us to rise in thunder, step where stars are strewn, pace the cold, black, desert dune of space, meander on the moon, then race back to planet Earth. Von Braun erupted energy like uranium atoms in fission. Ideas popped in his mind like flashbulbs.

In the late summer of 1976 I was stunned to learn that von Braun was stricken with cancer. The news served as a catalyst to jolt my mind into action. For a long time I had been dreaming of collecting into one book the accounts of the outstanding men of our space age who had zoomed God into focus in the minds of millions.

The one thing that has impressed me most about our space age, next to the actual landing on the moon, is the fact that as a group the men of our space age have been men of faith and prayer who were not afraid to stand before the cameras of the world and publicly profess their belief in God and in the power of prayer.

First and foremost of these men is Dr. Wernher von Braun himself. No space-age scientist I know of has done as much as von Braun to bring God to the attention of millions. Because of von Braun's many inspiring statements pertaining to religion, I have quoted him more often than anyone else in my science classes, my Sunday sermons, and in my various science books and pamphlets.

I would like to share with you some of my memories of von Braun, and then let him speak to you himself through quotations he has given me permission to use.

The name of von Braun first appeared on my horizon immediately following World War II when he accepted a contract from the United States Army to work on our fledgling rocket program. Before long, under his guidance, the White Sands Missile Range in New Mexico vibrated to the earth-jarring thunders of rocket engines as V-2s and Wac-Corporal rockets leaped into the sky.

My second year of teaching at Campion High School, Prairie du Chien, Wisconsin, was a vintage year for von Braun and his team. In that year, 1949, they successfully launched a two-stage rocket to an altitude of 250 miles.

In 1950 the army moved von Braun and his team to Huntsville, Alabama. Dr. von Braun was named technical director. Emphasis was on creation of ballistic missile systems for defense, but von Braun had his eyes on outer space. He pressed in vain, however, for authority to attempt a satellite launch.

Among my cherished treasures are copies of the now-defunct *Colliers* magazine in which von Braun pleaded with America to wake up to the possibility of using a rocket to place a man on the moon. Alas, only a few technical people could foresee what was coming in space. Just a few years earlier, in December 1945, Dr. Vannevar Bush, the wartime leader of military technology, told a Senate committee: "There has been a great deal of talk about a three-thousand-mile, high-angle rocket, shot from one continent to another, carrying an atomic bomb, and so directed to be a precise weapon which would land exactly on a certain target such as a city.

"I say, technically I don't think anybody in this world knows how to do such a thing, and I feel confident it will not be done for a very long period of time to come. I think we can leave that out of our thinking. I wish the American people would leave it out of their thinking."

The United States was jolted in August 1957, when the Soviet Union announced that it had test-fired a multistage, intercontinental missile. It was the "impossible" weapon Vannevar Bush had urged Americans just twelve years earlier to forget.

Never will I forget the shock of horror that swept over the United States on October 4, 1957, when we heard on our radios the first "beep-beep" coming from space. To our dismay, we learned that the Soviet Union had put *Sputnik*, the first man-made satellite into orbit.

The Soviet Union lost no time in informing the world that it was now able to deliver a great package of nuclear destruction to every part of the United States, and that this could be done without leaving Russian soil.

On October 7, the Soviet Union announced that it had successfully tested a "mighty hydrogen warhead of a new design." The chilling message was perfectly clear. The Soviet Union had become the number one military power and could utilize space to deliver weapons of mass destruction to any part of the world. The tremors that raced

Scientist-astronaut Harrison Schmitt collects rock samples from the moon's surface with a lunar rake. Collecting rocks, however, was not our primary purpose for going to the moon. (NASA photo)

around the world were not recorded on the Richter scale, but they shook the minds of men.

Arthur C. Clarke, a well-known British space expert, said: "As of Saturday [October 4, 1957] the United States became a second-rate power."

Dr. Theodor Heuss, president of West Germany, sought to calm his people with an appeal not to succumb to "a wave of hysteria."

A spokesman in Egypt said that the orbiting of *Sputnik* "will make countries think twice before tying themselves to the imperialist policy of the United States."

I recall only too vividly the days and weeks that followed *Sputnik*. Again and again, people in all walks of life, including my students, asked the same questions: Will Russia drop an atom bomb on us now? Is there any hope for us? What can the United States do now?

Senator Richard Russell of Georgia, chairman of the Armed Services Committee, said: "*Sputnik* confronts America with a new and terrifying military danger."

To some people, indeed, *Sputnik* was as intimidating as if the Russians had placed an atomic bomb in orbit. Its impact was not lost on the world or on the American public.

Nineteen years after *Sputnik*, during the bicentennial year of 1976, I was amazed when my students would ask: "Why did we spend billions of dollars to make rockets to go to the moon?"

The question was asked in a quizzical mood that seemed to imply that we spent twenty-four billion dollars just so a small, select group of rock hounds could have a picnic in space and pick up some odd-shaped rocks from the surface of our nearest companion in space.

Anyone who lived through the terror of the post-*Sputnik* days and the bullying threats of Russia should recall that we did not enter the space race primarily to make the dream of moon travel come true. We did so in the interests of national defense. We knew that any nation that

America's first satellite, Explorer, was put into orbit on January 31, 1958. (United States Army photo)

had a rocket powerful enough to go to the moon could use such a rocket to drop atomic bombs anywhere on earth.

Commenting on the post-*Sputnik* era, staff writers of *U.S. News & World Report*, who compiled the superb book *U.S. on the Moon*, said: "The core of worldwide concern was in the area of military security. Whether we liked it or not, we were now involved in a space race — not because we sought or desired such a race, but simply because if we refrained from entering it the Soviet Union would inevitably extend its sway over a greater part of the world. Of that there was little doubt in the minds of serious men in the United States, Europe, Latin America, the Middle East, Asia, and Africa."

In recent years I was given a new insight into national defense when I visited the Strategic Air Command Post at Offutt Air Force Base, just south of Omaha, Nebraska. At the entrance to the post is a huge, billboard-type sign that says, PEACE IS OUR PROFESSION.

A booklet informs the visitor: "Although SAC represents the most powerful striking force in the world's history, the command's primary mission is not to fight but to preserve peace. SAC's strength is such that no sane enemy would dare attack us because of the risk of retaliation from SAC's bombers and missiles."

"Our power, however," said the air force chief of staff, "will be sufficient deterrent only so long as it convinces potential enemies that aggression against us is profitless."

Back in the dark days of the autumn of 1957, we did not have "sufficient deterrent." In that dark hour of public humiliation and fear, the nation hurried to the doorstep of the one man who could help America lift itself out of the quagmire. It was a moment of supreme irony. The United States government came running to the man against whom it had earlier closed its ears. Von Braun's past articles in *Colliers* took on a prophetic tone. For long years he had been telling us that we could have been the first in space, but no one seemed to take him at his word. After years of being the target of skeptics who, like dart players, hurled their needle-sharp objections into his skin, von Braun had every justification to stand back in injured dignity and shout, "I told you so!"

It is a glowing tribute to von Braun's greatness that he wasted no time in self-pity. He leaped eagerly to the job at hand.

Dr. von Braun knew exactly what had to be done. Almost all his life he had dreamed of the day when he could work on a space rocket. He had made reams of exquisitely precise calculations.

An incredibly brief eighty-four days after the go-ahead, von Braun and his team tasted success. On January 31, 1958, *Explorer 1*, America's first satellite, was put in orbit. Although *Explorer 1* weighed only thirty-one pounds, this tiny moonlet announced to the world that America had entered the space age.

The National Space Act of 1959, creating the National Aeronautics and Space Administration (NASA), opened a new era for Dr. von Braun. He and his associates were assigned to staff NASA's George C. Marshall Space Flight Center in Huntsville, Alabama.

On April 12, 1961, the world had another shock. The Soviet Union announced an incredible feat. It had placed a man in orbit around the earth for the first time in history. The flight of Yuri Gagarin in a five-ton spacecraft called *Vostok* demonstrated that the Russians not only were developing the rocket power for lifting greater weights into orbit than the United States could launch, but had been able to perfect a vehicle that could take a human being into space and return him safely to earth. *Vostok* again demonstrated the superiority of the Soviet Union in space, touching off another wave of apprehension throughout the non-Communist world.

Space now became one of the major preoccupations of John F. Kennedy, the thirty-fifth president of the United States. On May 25, 1961, in his second State of the Union address, President Kennedy announced the decision to go to the moon. In his address, Kennedy made it clear that the purpose of the moon mission was both political and military. "If we are to win the battle that is now going on around the world between freedom and tyranny," President Kennedy said, "the dramatic achievements in space which occurred in recent weeks should have made clear to us all, as did *Sputnik* in 1957, the impact of this adventure on the minds of men everywhere who are attempting to make a determination of which road they should take."

According to Theodore C. Sorensen, then a White House aide, "The President was more convinced than any of his advisers that a second-rate, second-place space effort was inconsistent with this country's security."

No longer did von Braun have to plead for a crack at space. As the director of NASA's Marshall Space Flight Center, he was now required to reach the moon.

On Thursday, November 9, 1967, on Cape Kennedy's Launchpad 39A, Dr. von Braun's dream came true. The mighty *Saturn 5* rocket leaped for the sky. It was an impressive demonstration that, after ten years, the United States had finally overtaken and surpassed Russia in brute rocket power.

The newspaper accounts of the *Saturn 5* launch were lyrical. "America jumped a double step ahead of Russia," a typical story began, "on the road to the moon Thursday with a magnificent maiden launch of its *Saturn 5* rocket and the safe return of a robot-manned *Apollo* capsule at lunar-mission speed."

The deputy director of the National Space Agency, Robert Seamans, said the *Saturn-Apollo* flight gave the United States the capability "to not only take on the lunar-landing program, but any other space objective this country feels it wants."

According to an article by Lawrence Lee, the *Saturn* shot worked like a dream, evaporating the gloom that had been haunting our space program. America could now hope — in the words of the motto of the Strategic Air Command — for PEACE THROUGH POWER.

On Christmas Eve of the following year, three Americans became the first astronauts to circle the moon. The next year, on Sunday, July 20, 1969, an American astronaut, Neil A. Armstrong, became the first man to walk on the surface of the moon.

Dr. Wernher von Braun proved to be a "savior" of the United States. He is the man most responsible for our success in space.

Though von Braun was "Father of the *Saturn*" and director of the George C. Marshall Space Flight Center, he was not a narrow-minded specialist. Rather, his range of interests and vision was as wide as humanity itself. He was truly a Renaissance man whose interests ran from music and science to education and theology.

Because of his outstanding ability and wide range of interests, he was frequently called upon to speak to various groups and to contribute articles to many publications. From his many public talks and numerous writings, I culled quotations, which I incorporated into my classes, my sermons, my science books, and other writings. Dr. Wernher von Braun was always most generous in giving me permission to quote from his material. In return for his generosity, I always sent him copies of the books and pamphlets in which I made use of his words and ideas.

Over a stretch of some twenty years, this has resulted in a lot of correspondence. Among my most cherished possessions are the letters I received from Dr. Wernher von Braun throughout our years of friendship.

My first hardcover book, in which I made reference to von Braun, was *Wonderland*, a science book for young people, published in 1958 by Loyola University Press, Chicago. This book has been out of print for many years.

My next hardcover book, *Adventures in Science*, a general science textbook of 677 pages, was published by Loyola University Press in 1963. Dr. Wernher von Braun was so delighted with the personal copy of the book I sent to him that he wrote to me in reply: "I am grateful for your courtesy in making available to me a copy of your general science textbook, *Adventures in Science;* and I congratulate you . . . . You have done truly yeoman service by turning the classroom into a launching pad of exciting new ideas to boost the minds of the young into orbits of knowledge and inspiration, remembering always that every advance in science, every achievement in technology, every master-piece of art comes from the mind."

Although I had the wonderful privilege of a heart-warming correspondence with von Braun over a span of many years, I deeply regret that I never had an opportunity to meet this magnificent man personally. The nearest thing to what might be called a roundabout, long-range introduction took place in the fall of 1967, just a few weeks before von Braun test-fired the *Saturn 5* rocket from Cape Kennedy.

For many years it was the custom at Campion High School, where I taught science for twenty-eight years, to have an open house in the early autumn for visiting parents, relatives, and friends. Visitors were invited to attend classes and see for themselves the teaching techniques in use at Campion. On that particular day I had an overflow crowd of visitors. Even standing room was at a premium.

After class, the uncle of one of my students introduced himself to me and mentioned that he was working with von Braun. The visitor went on to say that he was so impressed by my science demonstrations that he would request von Braun to send me a photo of the upcoming *Saturn 5* launch.

Imagine my delight some weeks after when I received a large color photo of the launch with this inscription: *To Father Scott: Best wishes to an inspiring science teacher.*

— Wernher von Braun

In midsummer of 1976 I sent von Braun a copy of my book *Phenomena of Our Universe.* As a rule von Braun would acknowledge receipt of any book I sent him within two or three weeks. As the summer crept past without a return letter, I began to suspect that something must have happened.

With deep sorrow I read a brief item in the newspaper informing me that von Braun was terminally ill with cancer in an Alexandria, Virginia, hospital.

A few days later, on September 1, 1976, I received this letter from his administrative assistant: "As you may know, Dr. von Braun is presently seriously sick and unable to handle his mail. However, he asked that I respond to your recent letter and extend his sincere thanks for the copy of your book which you forwarded him. Dr. von Braun also asked that I forward you the enclosed copy of his latest paper, which he hopes you will enjoy.

"Finally, Dr. von Braun asked that I convey his warmest personal regards and to let you know he is most honored with the high esteem you hold for his work."

Dr. Wernher von Braun was much more than "the Father of the *Saturn*"; he was an apostle of truth, of beauty, and of love. Like all truly great men, von Braun was humble. In the very first paragraph of the talk he had written to deliver to the Lutheran Church of America in Philadelphia on October 29, 1976, Dr. von Braun said: "When President Marshall invited me to this symposium and suggested that I present my thoughts on responsible scientific investigation and application, I wondered whether I was really up to this task. Science, after all, has many facets and I have had only a limited view of a very few of them."

This sentiment of von Braun's echoes that of Sir Isaac Newton, one of the greatest scientists of all ages. The world paid Sir Isaac Newton great honor for all he did to bring new ideas to light. Yet, in spite of his great knowledge, here is what Newton said of himself: "To myself I seem to have been only like a boy playing on the seashore and diverting myself in now and then finding a smoother

21

pebble or a prettier shell than ordinary, whilst the great ocean of truth lay all undiscovered before me."

Thomas Alva Edison put it more bluntly: "We don't know one millionth of one percent about anything."

Some years ago, in a commencement address delivered at St. Louis University, von Braun reminded his audience that "Nature around us still harbors many thousands of times more unsolved than solved mysteries."

In a newspaper article that appeared on July 30, 1966, von Braun said: "Scientific discoveries have come at an ever-increasing pace, for the truth is not static. For every new answer, a dozen new questions spring up. Science is facing wide-open frontiers in many fields; the atomic nucleus is becoming more and more enigmatic; the origin and structure of the universe are still shrouded in mystery; and the exact bodily functions of living organisms still evade complete understanding."

On May 6, 1970, Dr. Wernher von Braun wrote me a personal note saying he was greatly honored that I had again quoted him. "I must confess," he added, "that I feel utterly inadequate to seriously address these problems that have moved the greatest thinkers since the dawn of time."

On Wednesday, June 15, 1977, at the age of sixty-five, died the world's greatest rocket expert, Dr. Wernher von Braun. The man who had become the rocket wizard of the twentieth century was born in Wirsitz, East Prussia, on March 23, 1912.

It was von Braun's mother who started him on his trip to the moon. An unusual woman, accomplished both as a musician and as an astronomer, she transmitted her enthusiasms to her son. Developing precocious skill on both the cello and the piano, for a while young Wernher thought he might pursue a musical career.

Astronomy proved to be the more lasting enthusiasm, especially after his mother, ignoring the precedent that called for a gold watch as a confirmation present, bought him a high-powered telescope instead. This was his point of departure on his long trek through the heavens. As a teenager, von Braun spent long hours with his telescope. "It filled me with a romantic urge to soar through the heavens," he said, "and actually explore the mysterious universe."

Describing von Braun as a "man of bold vision," President Carter remarked that: "To millions of Americans, Wernher von Braun's name was inextricably linked to our exploration of space and the creative application of technology. Not just the people of our nation, but all the people of the world have profited from his work. We will continue to profit from his example."

THE UNIVERSE ACCORDING TO VON BRAUN

It is refreshing as mountain dew to glimpse the universe from the viewpoint of Wernher von Braun. He reminds us that, from concept to countdown, the entire Apollo project was an incredible achievement.

He reminds us how dazzled and amazed we were when we switched on the TV to watch *Saturn 5* rockets leaping to the moon. We were fascinated still more when we watched TV pictures of our astronauts driving a car over the surface of the moon.

Yet, the greatest thing of all is that our adventures into space have confirmed our belief in God, and given us new glimpses into His beauty and skill.

Listen, now, as Dr. Wernher von Braun explains his views: "The natural laws of the universe are so precise that we have no difficulty building a spaceship to fly to the moon, and we can time the flight with a precision of a fraction of a second.

"These laws must have been set by somebody.

"Anything as well ordered and perfectly created as is our earth and universe must have a Maker, a Master Designer. Anything so orderly, so perfect, so precisely balanced, so majestic as this creation can only be the product of a Divine Idea.

"There must be a Maker; there can be no other way.

"Finite man cannot comprehend an omnipresent, omniscient, omnipotent, and infinite God. Any effort to visualize God, to reduce Him to our comprehension, to describe Him in our language, beggars His greatness."

How inspiring it is to listen to Dr. Wernher von Braun proclaim his faith in God as our Father. And since God is our Father, all of us are His children; hence, we should treat each other with love and respect as becomes the children of God.

"My relationship with God," said the Father of the U.S. Space Program, "is very personal. I think you can be on first name terms with Him, you know, and tell Him what your troubles are, and ask for help. I do it all the time, and it works for me."

Today science dominates our lives as never before. Electron microscopes make it possible for us to look into the world of the ultrasmall. The thrust of rockets has made it possible for man to explore the universe beyond the earth. An X-ray telescope mounted on an orbiting observatory called *Einstein* has radioed back an image of Cygnus X-1, a star system thought to contain one of space's black holes.

Even as you read this page, two spacecraft are hurtling through space. After exploring Jupiter and Saturn, the *Voyager* twins are destined to leave the solar system and wander billions of years through the stars.

Just in case another race should come upon the *Voyager* spacecraft a couple of eons from now, a message was sent on a gold-plated record, encoding 117 photographs as well as greetings in fifty-five languages, plus hellos from the president of the United States, the secretary general of the United Nations, and an anonymous humpback whale.

According to von Braun, religion is as important and dynamic as science: "We should remember that science exists only because there are people, and its concepts exist only in the minds of men. Behind these concepts lies reality — revealed to us only by the grace of God.

"While science seeks control over the forces of nature around us, religion controls the forces of nature within us.

"As we learn more and more about nature, we become more deeply impressed and humbled by its orderliness and unerring perfection. Our expanding knowledge of the laws of the universe has enabled us to send men out of their natural environment into the strange new environment of space and return them safely to earth."

According to von Braun, it is God who, through the imperceptible goadings of sense-beauty, penetrates our hearts in order to make our life flow out into His own.

God comes down into us by means of a tiny scrap of created reality; and then, suddenly, He unfurls His immensity before our eyes, and displays Himself to us.

In the life springing up within us, in the material elements that sustain us, it is not just the gifts of God we discern, it is God Himself we encounter. It is God who causes us to share in His own being. His hands mold us. Every presence should make us feel that God is near us. Every touch is the touch of His hand.

We should bathe ourselves in the ocean of matter, plunge into it where it is deepest and most violent, struggle in its currents, and drink of its waters. It is that ocean that will raise us up to God. Till the very end of time matter will always remain young, exuberant, sparkling, new-born — for those who are open to seeing it in this way.

Von Braun was fond of quoting from Kant — "Two things never fail to spark my utmost admiration: the starry sky above me and the moral law within me."

In the talk which he had prepared to give on October 29, 1976, von Braun said: "I am not in despair about the discordant conditions of our social environment. In spite of all the temporary setbacks that humanity has suffered through the centuries, and the terrible things that have happened in our times, I strongly believe that God, in the same personal relationships He established through Jesus Christ, will see to it that man's path will continue upward leading toward gradual improvement."

Von Braun tells us to view the universe as both lovable and loving. He interprets Christ's teachings on the overriding importance of love and charity as not just desirable virtues but as fundamental forces in the nature of God's creation. With utmost accuracy von Braun says that the power of love is the "most precious gift with which God endowed His creation."

How very true. The sky is never so blue and the meadowlark never sings so sweetly as when we are overflowing with love. A man in love can say to the queen of his heart, "This is a lovelier world because of you."

Love lights fuses in your veins. It ignites skyrockets that cascade showers of golden sparks. It unleashes Roman candles lancing the darkness of the night.

According to Franz Weyergan, "If you have not known the temptation to see in one beloved face the whole glory of God, you have not known love."

Harold Blake Walker informs us that if we look for God only in some shattering mystical experience, we are likely to miss Him in the warmth of caring human relationships, wherein He is most surely to be found.

"He who abides in love," said St. John, "abides in God, and God in him."

"I encounter God," says Father Ellwood Kieser, "in the one I love. I feel Him in the electricity that sings between us. I know Him in the mysterious fashion which takes place when two souls touch."

We begin our communion with God when we become alive to human warmth and human love.

Von Braun brings out the fact that today we are told that one of the most important things in religion is an understanding of love. If a man does not know how to love, how can he know much about the God who is Love?

Since all true love comes from God, man becomes a lover of God when he enters into the experience of true love.

All of us hunger for sharing life with others. This opens to us as nothing else does the sharing of life with God Himself.

No doubt you have heard people say that they have trouble with their faith because they cannot visualize God. The answer von Braun gives to this objection is superb. "Can a physicist visualize an electron?" he asks. "The electron is materially inconceivable, and yet it is so perfectly known through its effects that we use it to illuminate our cities, guide our airliners through the night skies, and take the most accurate measurements.

"What strange rationale makes some physicists accept the inconceivable electron as real while refusing to accept the reality of God on the ground that they cannot conceive Him?"

How strange to realize that the electron has never been seen by man. We believe in it for the same reason we should believe in God — because of the effects we notice in the universe around us.

Perhaps you object that when you turn on your electric light you "see electricity." The truth is that we never see the electrons forcing their way through the tungsten wire that makes up the filament of the lamp.

Do you know why the light bulbs in your home are called *incandescent lamps*? The word *incandescent* means *glowing white-hot*. And this is exactly what happens. The electricity going through the very thin wires, or filaments, in the lamps makes them glow white-hot, so they give off light as well as heat.

"But," you may object, "I most certainly see electrons in motion when I see a flash of lightning."

When you look at a lightning flash, you do not see electricity itself. All you see is a burning spark channel or burning column of air which may be about an inch in diameter, or even as thin as a hair on your head. The path of this burning air column may be as long as ten miles. The searing, 3,000-degree heat of the flash causes the channel of air to expand or explode with tremendous force. The airwave thus produced pounds against your eardrum to cause the sensation we call thunder. If the discharge is close by, the thunder comes as a sharp, whiplike crack.

The comments of von Braun on the unseen electron may be made even more vivid for you if you consider the following. Let me begin by asking, "What are you looking at this moment?"

"I'm looking at print on this paper," you reply. Your answer seems clear-cut, definite, and final. The scientist, however, will inform you that your answer has not even dipped into the magic, mystery, and fascination that swirls through this page.

According to atomic theory, this print, this paper, even the tip of your ear, and indeed your whole body, are made of atoms.

Atoms — so the theory goes — are like tiny solar systems made up of protons and electrons. The protons are in the center of the atom just as our sun is in the center of our solar system. Electrons revolve around the protons as planets revolve around our sun.

A negative charge of electricity is called an electron and is designated by a minus sign (−).

A positive charge of electricity is called a proton and is designated by a plus sign (+).

What, now, do scientists ask you to believe? That this paper is made up of electrical charges of electricity, which we designate by (−) signs and (+) signs. Yet, you and I and the scientist know that *if* we could climb down into the heart of an atom, we certainly would never expect to find plus signs and minus signs running around.

I'm quite sure that, even if I were endowed with the powers of the Six-Million-Dollar Man or the Bionic Woman and had a supermicroscope that would enable me to look down into my skin, I would *not* find a bunch of minus signs. *Just what* would I see? What does an electron look like? No one knows. We are lost in mystery. We are so *ignorant* of what an atom really is, so *ignorant* of what electricity is, that we have to resort to the clumsy use of a minus sign (−) to represent what we call an electron, and a plus sign (+) to represent what we call a proton.

Hence, these symbols, the plus sign (+) and the minus sign (−), may be said to be *symbols of our ignorance!*

Since we don't *know* what an atom really is, we invent a *theory*, which is nothing but an educated guess.

The most popular and best-known theory of the atom today is the Bohr theory, named after the famed Niels Bohr, Nobel prize winner. This is the theory we have just considered. Today, however, there are scientists who wish to introduce changes into Bohr's theory.

Isaac Asimov, the well-known writer on science, reminds us that "nobody can say what the inside of an atom looks like. Conditions are so different within the atom from the conditions found in the ordinary world about us that we have nothing that will serve as a true comparison."

When you look at your thumb or big toe, perhaps you see nothing that strikes you as romantic or mysterious. To the atomic scientist, however, each square centimeter of your skin and, indeed, of your whole body, is teeming with mystery.

Each cell in your body is a "universe in miniature" — a fascinating world of "planet" electrons whirling around protons.

Von Braun would agree with the sentiment of Nehru: "We live in a wonderful world that is full of beauty and charm and adventure. There is no end to the adventures that we can have if only we seek them with our eyes open."

The universe is full of magical things — patiently waiting for our senses to grow sharper so that we may discover them. Every morning we should lean awhile on the windowsill of heaven and gaze upon the Lord.

It is interesting to note that Dr. Wernher von Braun was not alone in reminding the world of the limitations of human knowledge.

Lee A. DuBridge has the authority, based on experience, that enables him to speak with confidence. He is president of the California Institute of Technology, the institution which manages the world-famous Jet Propulsion Laboratory for the National Aeronautics and Space Administration. "I could easily spend fifty years studying about the universe," said Lee DuBridge, "and still not know all I'd like to know."

"Why?"

"For one simple reason: If I really were intent on learning all there was to know about physics, for example, or astronomy, or biology, or economics, or philosophy, I would soon come to some question for which *nobody* had an answer.

"How many elementary particles are there? *Nobody knows.*

"How does the DNA molecule govern the development of a newborn creature? No one fully knows. Why do men and nations always fight each other? *We don't know! We don't know!*"

One of the most outstanding scientists of our times is Dr. Charles H. Townes, who won the Nobel prize for his work that led to the laser. Listen now to the words of Dr. Townes that echo those of von Braun: "We know that the most sophisticated present scientific theories, including modern quantum mechanics, are still incomplete. We use them because in certain areas they are so amazingly right. Yet they lead us at times into inconsistencies which we do not understand, and where we must recognize that we have missed some crucial ideas. We simply admit and accept the paradoxes and hope that sometime in the future they will be resolved by a more complete understanding."

Here, now, are golden words from Dr. Charles Townes. He tells us that in both religion and science "we

31

must expect paradoxes, and not be surprised or unduly troubled by them.

"We know of paradoxes in physics," continues Dr. Townes, "such as that concerning the nature of light. In the realm of religion, we are troubled by the suffering around us, and its apparent inconsistency with a God of love.

"Such paradoxes do not destroy our faith. They simply remind us of a limited understanding, and at times provide a key to learning more."

Werner Heisenberg is considered one of the great pioneers of modern physics. When some of his assertions brought him into conflict with Einstein, physicists rose to take sides in the dispute.

Following Heisenberg's death in early 1976, the intellectual struggle between Heisenberg and Einstein, which had continued for many years, was "resolved" by most physicists taking the middle view that some intimate workings of nature will indeed remain unknowable and unpredictable.

Dr. James A. Van Allen is the famed scientist who discovered the Van Allen radiation belts that surround the earth, and which were named in his honor. "At the frontier of science," says Dr. Van Allen, "the effort is subjective, intuitive, controversial, sometimes courageous, often misdirected, often inconclusive, often plain wrong. It is anything but exact."

One of the hallmarks of great men in modern science is their humility when confronted with the mysteries of nature. And this is true not only in the space sciences but in other sciences as well.

By reputation and accomplishment, Dr. Lewis Thomas is a leader in the field of medical practice and research. He is the author of an acclaimed series of essays on man and nature, life and death, sickness and health. His book *The Lives of a Cell: Notes of a Biology Watcher* won the 1975 National Book Award in arts and letters.

Currently president of the Memorial Sloan-Kettering Cancer Center, Dr. Lewis was formerly dean of the Yale Medical School, and before that chairman of the departments of pathology and medicine and dean at the New York University-Bellevue Medical Center.

Here, now, are the words of a man who is researching as well as administering one of the country's prestigious medical centers: "I am a mystified man. I don't really understand very much."

The uncertainty over the disputed items in science reaches down into our daily lives. For years now, the experts have been arguing over the feasibility of using nuclear power to light and heat our cities. Is it too dangerous? Or is the use of nuclear power, in fact, the only intelligent solution to our chronic energy crisis? "How can the public decide," a recent *Time* magazine article asks, "when even the scientists disagree?" There is no easy way to sort out the truth in arguments between scientists.

How did von Braun face the argument that many modern evolutionists believe that the universe is the arbitrary result of random arrangements and rearrangements of uncounted atoms and molecules over billions of years?

Dr. Wernher von Braun's reply is exact and to the point. "Take the evolution of the eye in the animal world," he says. "What random process could possibly explain the simultaneous evolution of the eye's optical system, the nervous conductors of the optical signals from the eye to the brain, and the optical nerve center in the brain itself where the incoming light impulses are converted to an image the conscious mind can comprehend?

"There is the even more mysterious interaction between animals and plants. We know that the eye of the honeybee cannot see red, but is sensitive to a band of ultraviolet light which the human eye cannot discern.

"Flowers, depending on visits by bees for their pollination, have developed intricate ultraviolet patterns designed to attract the bee's attention.

"Did the flowers fashion the bee's eye, or did the bees, through limiting their visits to a few flowers which, through random mutation, happened to have these attractive ultraviolet patterns, ensure their survival as the fittest for bees?

"Let us be honest and let us be humble: Can all this really be explained without the notion of a Divine Intent, without a Creator?

"Also, it is one thing to accept natural order as a way of life, but the minute one asks 'Why?' then again enter God and all His glory."

Each day we live in a world throbbing with romance, adventure, mystery, and fascination, a world teeming with hints of a Reality beyond phenomena. All we need do is open the windows of our mind, and we shall perceive with Gerard Manley Hopkins:

The world is charged with the grandeur of God. . . .
Nature is never spent . . .
Because the Holy Ghost over the bent
World broods with warm breast and with ah! bright wings.

In a beautiful and inspiring address to the Catholic Library Association of Ontario, Edith K. Peterkin said, "The whole of education is preparation for the beatific vision. The whole world is a holy encounter."

God is, indeed, present in all the beauty of creation. Mathematics teaches us something of the mind of the Maker. Biology, chemistry, and physics show us God's deep design in creation. All the lessons, be they geography or literature, bear the imprint of the words, "I am a God, who loves."

"The world is a miraculous chrysalis," says Dr. Jonathan Miller, "which cracks open under the heat of attention."

Saint Patrick, centuries ago, summarized much of

what I have been trying to say in his prayer, or creed, known as "The Breastplate of Saint Patrick":

I arise today
In the might of heaven:
Splendor of the sun,
Whiteness of the moon,
Irresistibleness of fire,
Swiftness of lightning,
Speed of the wind,
Absoluteness of the deep,
Earth's stability,
Rock's durability.
I arise today:
In the might of God for my piloting.

It is interesting to note that more honors came to Dr. Wernher von Braun than to any other space-age man; yet they sat lightly on his six-foot frame, and he refused to fall captive to the legends that surrounded him.

When von Braun came on the scene, he unwittingly dominated it by virtue of an ineffable something called star quality, compounded of his contagious warmth and manifest confidence, his logic and clarity in articulating ideas, the lightness with which he wore his honors, his sparkling witticisms, never cruel and always pertinent. He was not coy about acknowledging his contributions to the conquest of space, but he did it without arrogance and insisted on sharing credit with colleagues and subordinates.

Like all disciplined scientists, von Braun was committed to the measurable and demonstrable and was obedient to the immutable laws of nature. He was also a deeply religious man.

Von Braun regarded his home as a retreat away from the scrutiny of the curious, a place to relax with Chopin, Puccini, or Mozart, and curl up with a book. Most of Dr. von Braun's reading related in some way to the sciences, but he enjoyed forays into subjects as disparate as philosophy and medieval history.

The spirit of von Braun is that expressed in "Praised Be Diversity" by Liam Brophy:

The Lord be praised for this diversity
That makes our world a place of long delight,
From pulsing stars to pushing seeds: from suns
Of island universes in the sea
Of His immensity,
To unseen atoms holding all the might
Of unimagined power; from wind that runs
About the round of the revolving earth
Shouting for very mirth,
To virgin silences of Arctic night;
For multitudinous miracles of sight
And sound and touch and smell; for speech
By which heart touches heart,
And all men reach
Beyond their loneliness; and for all art
By which dead hands have hung upon our days
Their dreams of deathless beauty; and for lays
That startle us with exquisite surprise
With memories of lost Paradise
Like sudden rumors of approaching spring
About retreating winter. Thankful praise
To Thee, O Lord, for everything
From tiny to tremendous; from the height
Of dazzling heavens to the utmost dark
Of ocean depths; for fur and skin and bark,
For every fold and fiber, grit and grain.
For every insect hum and whir of wings,
And wash of waves; for ecstasy and pain;
For roadway rumblings;
For dunes of snow and laughter of the sun
On waterfalls; for things shining and dun;
For baby cheeks, and the serrated crest

Of everlasting hills;
For riotous rain that fills
The dusty dikes; for toil and rest;
For youth and age, but most of all for love
And laughter of true friends
That, like the power of the protecting Dove,
Holds the world's ends.
We lift our separate hearts in praise of Thee;
I think we may
Spend heaven's timeless, tideless, changeless day
In praise of these devices and the way
Of Thy remembered dear diversity.

HE JUMPED 19 MILES

How often do you pick up a national magazine and find in it a story of a man who proclaims his faith in God and the power of prayer?

You can imagine my surprise, therefore, a number of years ago, when I picked up a copy of the *National Geographic* magazine for December 1960 and found the account of a man who made public profession of the fact that he prays.

This man who proclaimed his faith before the world is Captain Joseph W. Kittinger. He had a unique and dangerous job to do in making possible our Apollo project.

Long before our astronauts blasted off from the Kennedy Space Center atop a *Saturn 5* rocket bound for the moon, they had to know for sure that their space suits would work when they touched down on the airless surface of the moon.

We planet people sometimes forget that we live at the bottom of a great sea, a sea of air over six hundred miles high, and weighing more than five quadrillion (five million billion) tons. When you cast a weather eye into the wild blue yonder, the air looks like a gauzy fabric spun of sapphire threads and turquoise gems. Who would ever imagine that all the blue ethereal sky is squeezing down on every square foot of your body with an overwhelming pressure of 2,016 pounds! The amazing fact is that, as we toddle around planet Earth wearing the water-filled space suits of our skins, we seldom stop to realize that we are prisoners in the middle of a gigantic tug of war!

The atmosphere is pushing in on us with a pressure of fifteen pounds per square inch. We aren't squashed because the air inside our body is pushing out with equal force.

If someone suddenly stole the blanket of air surrounding us, the air trapped inside our bodies would expand and explode, dispatching our epidermises to all points of the compass.

A man on the moon would have to wear a pressurized space suit. If our man on the moon stumbled and ripped open his pressurized space suit, he would be exposed instantaneously to the lunar vacuum.

His fate was dramatized by a spectactular space experiment. A first-stage *Saturn* rocket took off from the Kennedy Space Center. Ninety miles above the earth, a hundred tons of water were suddenly released.

Dr. Wernher von Braun reported that the water literally exploded, expanding in all directions at a speed of more than a mile a second.

Thus it seems possible that any substantial tear in a space suit would cause death by explosive vaporization of all the explorer's body fluids.

To forestall such tragedy, engineers designed a suit sturdy enough to withstand any accident. This suit was worn, not only by the astronauts on the moon, but also by those in orbit around planet Earth. If their spacecraft were to rupture, they would have to depend on their survival equipment to bring them back alive to planet Earth.

When the spacecraft sped back to planet Earth, our astronauts depended, in part, on parachutes to slow them down before they splashed into the ocean.

One man who was engaged in research for survival equipment was Captain Joseph W. Kittinger. His job was to learn the factors involved in high-altitude escape and to test equipment for high-altitude fliers faced with an emergency return to planet Earth.

At 3:30 A.M. on the morning of August 16, 1960, in the Tularosa Valley of New Mexico, Kittinger was helped into a partial pressure suit for the near-vacuum of over a hundred thousand feet. Without this protective suit, his blood would bubble like champagne.

Not far from the dressing trailer, a giant balloon was being inflated. The huge bag, so lifeless and formless on the prairie, began to take life and mounted to the sky like a giant sunflower. Finally the onion-shaped balloon reached to a height of 360 feet, as tall as a thirty-three-story building.

While the balloon was being inflated, Kittinger had time to reflect on the dangerous task ahead of him. To those who wondered how he could enjoy any degree of equanimity in view of the task before him, Kittinger replied that this attitude was based on his four-point viewpoint:

I must have confidence in my team.
I must have confidence in my equipment.
I must have confidence in myself.
I must have confidence in God.

Kittinger went on to say that, with such an outlook, a man can face almost anything.

Takeoff time was set for 5:30 A.M. Kittinger stepped into the gondola fastened to the balloon. The straps holding it were released, and the eager balloon leaped skyward at the rate of twelve hundred feet per minute. At fifty thousand feet the temperature fell to −94° Fahrenheit. At sixty thousand feet the balloon began to rise even more rapidly, some thirteen hundred feet per minute.

One hour and thirty-one minutes after the balloon left the New Mexico desert, it reached its peak altitude of 102,800 feet. At this height of some nineteen miles above

Captain Joseph W. Kittinger tests the seating arrangement in the gondola that was later attached to a giant balloon that lifted him some nineteen miles into the sky. (United States Air Force official photo)

the surface of the earth, Kittinger looked out from his perch and noticed something strange and beautiful. The blue sky that is so common to us rose only to some fifteen degrees above the horizon. From there on up the sky became increasingly dark until it became like the darkness of midnight around the balloon.

Now came the big moment in Kittinger's life. He had to jump, or fall, into space. He was only too aware of the sign fastened beneath the gondola door: HIGHEST STEP IN THE WORLD.

Kittinger knew only too well that if his pressure suit or helmet should fail, his blood would boil, his lungs rupture. Death would be only seconds away.

In the eerie silence of space, Kittinger knew that his life depended entirely upon his equipment, his own actions, and God. At X-minus-seventy-seconds Kittinger dropped the trailing antenna, cutting communications with the ground crew. Then he started the automatic cameras in the gondola to record his fall. At count zero he opened the door of the gondola. "Lord, take care of me now," he prayed, then stepped into space.

Captain Kittinger holds the record for the longest fall in history. His return from the edge of earth took thirteen minutes, forty-five seconds. His maximum speed was 614 miles an hour.

When Kittinger first began his fall, he was facing the earth. Then he rolled over on his back and discovered a most unusual sight. It was 7:12 A.M. He was flooded in the golden rays of the morning sun, yet high above him the silvery, pear-shaped balloon sparkled against a jet-black sky. He looked for stars but could not find them.

At twenty-one thousand feet above the earth, Kittinger's body plunged into a heavy blanket of clouds that cut off his vision. A few seconds later his main chute opened and Kittinger said a prayer as he was approaching the earth: "Thank you, Lord, for taking care of me during that long fall."

Finally, at an altitude of fifteen thousand feet, Kittinger fell free from the clouds, and within seconds landed amidst the sand, salt grass, and sage of the New Mexico desert.

In looking back over his experience, Captain Joseph W. Kittinger said that he realizes full well how dependent we all are upon God in our search for knowledge and truth.

X-15

Can you tell me the name of a man who, though given astronaut's wings, did not blast off for outer space atop a *Saturn 5* rocket?

The man is Major Robert White. On the morning of July 17, 1962, he climbed into the cockpit of the bullet-nosed experimental rocket plane, the *X-15*, a hybrid creation, half plane, half missile. It shared some things in common with the test model of the space shuttle.

Perhaps you may recall seeing on TV the first flight of the space shuttle. It was given a piggyback ride into space atop an airplane. The *X-15* was also boosted into space, but, instead of riding piggyback, it was hooked underneath the right wing of a B-52, then "mother and son" zoomed off into the sky to an altitude of fifty thousand feet. At this height Robert White flicked a switch releasing the shackles that held the *X-15* beneath the wing of the giant mother ship. With the thrust of its own rocket engines, the *X-15* soared to a height of slightly under fifty miles — 246,700 feet to be exact.

At this moment Robert White qualified as an astronaut — one who had crossed the invisible line into outer space. He glanced out the cockpit window and was thrilled to notice the curvature of the earth. Far to the south he could see the Gulf of Mexico, and then, on the other side, San Francisco Bay. Behind the bay he saw the Pacific Ocean with sunlight breaking in galaxies of diamonds against the sapphire swells.

Plunging back into the heavy atmosphere, the *X-15* changed color from somber black to black and red. Its nose and leading edges of its stubby wings glowed brightly. The tremendous friction with the air heated the outer portions of the *X-15* to over a thousand degrees.

Minutes later White landed on a dry lake near the Edwards Air Force Base in California. Parts of the plane were still smoldering when it landed.

The late President John Kennedy invited Robert White to the White House and presented him with the prized Robert J. Collier Award.

The next honor came to him in the Pentagon when the air force chief of staff, General Curtis LeMay, pinned the astronaut's wings on Major White. The general hailed White as the forerunner of a "new breed of pilots" who will one day fly into space routinely from standard airports.

General LeMay must have been gifted with prophetic powers when he foretold of that new breed of pilots. I have on my desk a copy of NASA's twentieth-anniversary book, which marks two decades of aerospace exploration and research. The book was issued in October 1978.

After listing the major achievements of the last twenty years, the book continues, "Beyond our twenty-first year we can see the shuttle evolving as the major factor in all our operations in space, facilitating and accelerating progress toward nearly all our goals."

According to the shuttle optimists, shuttle pilots will be making routine flights in the not-too-distant future. Current plans call for building five of the $500-million shuttles, each capable of about a hundred round trips into space. By the year 1985, NASA hopes to be making up to sixty round trips every twelve months. In flight, the shuttles will be capable of a dazzling array of *Star Trek*-ish functions, from repair work on existing satellites to the construction of solar power stations. Each ship can carry five crew members in addition to two pilots.

Much of the work of the shuttle in the first three years will be strictly scientific. By 1983, NASA hopes to be able to establish a permanently floating ninety-five-inch telescope at a height of a hundred miles, giving astronomers a better view of the heavens than they get from any earthbound telescope. And ten European nations are prepared to finance an entire space laboratory in which scientists with minimal space training will be able to live and carry out experiments in a zero-gravity, shirt-sleeve environment.

Robert White experiences a sense of personal satisfaction from the part he played in our aerospace age. He is thankful for the many honors bestowed upon him. He recalls with special satisfaction the award he was given at Villanova University — the Mendel Medal. This award, named for Father Gregor Mendel, discoverer of the laws of heredity, is given to outstanding scientists who are members in good standing of the Catholic Church.

Despite all his awards, Robert White is surprisingly casual about his role in the space program. "We still have a long way to go," he says frankly. "What the future will hold, no one can say for sure."

Major White has an air of quiet self-control and the slow, deliberate manner of speaking usually associated with people from the wide-open spaces. White actually is a New York City boy. He grew up in Ascension Parish on West 107th St., on the rim of Harlem. Although he lived close to the turbulence of the big city, he was lucky. "The Police Athletic League," says White, "gave me a chance which no amount of gratitude can fully repay. It kept us busy and out of mischief. If I can help youngsters now, perhaps I'll be paying off a small installment on the debt I owe."

At the age of eighteen, White entered the Army Air Force. He got his pilot's wings and second lieutenant's commission on February 7, 1944, and soon afterwards was sent overseas to England as a P-51 pilot with the 355th fighter group of the Eighth Air Force.

All told, he flew fifty-two combat missions and won eight Air Medals. Early in 1945, on a fighter sweep over Bavaria, he was shot down when a shell made a direct hit on his engine.

White, who was leading the attack, was the only one shot down. His experience in a series of prisoner of war camps helped him to crystallize his faith in God.

"In my earlier years," said White, "I had been inclined to take religion a bit casually. In the prisoner of war camps, I finally saw the light. It wasn't sudden or dramatic or anything like that. Cut off from everything that you know and love, you start to ask yourself questions."

As Allied successes mounted and the tide of war turned against the Nazis, the situation in the camp worsened to the point where prisoners were getting only a piece of black bread and a can of unpalatable soup a day.

White suggested that the prisoners "start to pray."

Pray they did, and the next morning a truck arrived from Switzerland with some Red Cross supplies, especially food. "You'll never be able to convince me that it wasn't providential," says White, "that it wasn't an answer to our prayers."

Over the years White's habit of turning to God in prayer grew stronger. There were many times when White says that prayer alone pulled him through a crisis.

Robert White and his wife, Doris, made religion the center of their home. They not only played with their children, they prayed with them, too.

White is convinced that through their example parents can guide their children and help them to develop a deep, spiritual faith. And faith, according to White, comes before anything else. "Material things," he says, "aren't all-important. A hundred years from now what will they all mean?"

White took sharp issue with Soviet cosmonaut Gherman Titov, who professed to see no evidence of God in outer space. According to White, Titov's intellect was rusty. Anyone with a clear mind can see that scientific discovery rolls back the doors of the unknown and leaves the human mind in awe at the vastness of the universe. Vast as it is, this world of scientific discovery is small in comparison with God's knowledge. "This," remarked White, "is what impresses me up there."

Astronaut White goes on to say that scientific curiosity and research only whet the mind's appetite for the vast world of eternity where knowledge is unlimited. "This excites me," says White, "and gives my work real meaning and depth."

14 13 12 11 10 9
8 7 6 **5** 4 3 2 1

WHAT SPACE TAUGHT
JOHN GLENN

Astronaut John Glenn became the first American to orbit earth when he made three turns around the globe, traveling 83,450 miles in four hours and fifty-six minutes.

Not everyone remembers that when John Glenn was a first lieutenant during WW II, he flew fifty-nine combat missions in the Pacific. He earned two Distinguished Flying Crosses and ten Air Medals in that global conflict.

In the Korean fighting, he shot down three Migs, earned two more DFCs and eight Air Medals while flying ninety missions. On July 16, 1957, he raced from NAS (Naval Air Station) Los Alamitos, California, to NAS Floyd Bennett Field, New York, in an F-8, earning another DFC. On that time-shattering hop, Glenn averaged 723 miles per hour, crossing the U.S. in three hours and twenty-two minutes.

The Reverend Frank Erwin, pastor of the Little Falls United Presbyterian Church of Arlington, Virginia, gives us some inside information on his most famous parishioner: "All the world knows of John Glenn the hero, of his quiet, steely courage. I want to tell of another John Glenn, the man of sincere and simple faith. If Americans could only share his faith, they might also share some of his courage to face the problems of their own daily lives.

"Some hide their belief in God," Pastor Erwin goes on, "as if it were a shabby thing. But John wears his Christian faith as easily as he wore his silvery space suit when he entered *Friendship 7*."

One spring John Glenn served as a youth counselor at a church camp in Westmorland Park, Virginia. He would give the teenagers Bible instruction, then teach them waterskiing on the Potomac.

Before going into training as an astronaut, John used to teach Sunday school. He was reluctantly forced to give it up because of the demands on his time.

Pastor Erwin said that he has never known John Glenn, when he was in town, to miss Sunday services. Usually he attends the early session, and in winter he often arrives early enough to help shovel snow off the walks.

Each night just before bedtime, the Glenn family (John, his wife, Annie, and their children, David and Lyn) gather around and read the Bible together. Each in turn reads a verse.

"When I was selected for the space program," says astronaut John Glenn, "one of the first things I was given was a booklet. This booklet, a space handbook put out by the Government Printing Office, contains a lot of information about our space program. But there was one paragraph that concerned the hugeness and vastness of the universe that impressed me very much."

John Glenn informs us that there is only one technical fact we have to know to be able to understand this particular paragraph. We must know what a light-year is.

The fastest traveler in all the universe is a beam of light. The cruising speed of the silver arrow that is light is 186,000 miles per second. At this speed a beam of light could dash back and forth between New York and Hollywood thirty-seven times per second. And if the light beam were a globe-trotter, it could zip around the earth seven times between heartbeats.

Even though the sun is some ninety-three million miles distant in space, it takes sunlight only some eight and a half minutes to make the trip. When you stretch out your hand to shake hands with a sunbeam, you are in contact with a cosmic traveler that left the flaming surface of the sun less than ten minutes ago.

If you could throw a saddle on a light beam, you would be in for the ride of your life. Each second you would gallop through the vastness of space at the devastating speed of 186,000 miles.

How far does light travel in one year? Multiply 186,000 miles per second by all the seconds in a year. The answer is approximately six trillion miles. This number, or the distance covered by a light beam in one year, is called a "light-year."

We live in what is called the Milky Way galaxy. Our galaxy contains some two hundred billion stars. From rim to rim, our galaxy is some hundred thousand light-years in diameter. Our sun is an insignificant star some thirty thousand light-years from the galactic center.

A light beam which travels from the sun to the earth in just over eight minutes takes a hundred thousand years to go from edge to edge of the Milky Way.

The earth and the entire solar system are actually a part of the Milky Way. Further, the solar system is just a tiny speck about two thirds of the distance from the center of the Milky Way galaxy. The entire galaxy, including the solar system, whirls around in space like a fiery pinwheel. Scientists estimate that the earth makes one revolution about the Milky Way every two hundred million years.

Beyond the Milky Way, at distances almost beyond man's understanding, are other galaxies, other universes that contain hundreds of millions of stars or suns. Only the galaxy Andromeda is visible to the unaided eye; telescopes are needed to see other galaxies. When photographed the galaxies appear as spiral nebulae or clouds. The spiral nebula in Andromeda is about nine hundred thousand light-years away. Galaxies more than a hundred million light-years distant have been observed through powerful telescopes.

Galaxies, including the Milky Way, have been compared to large islands in a tremendous ocean of space. The average distance between galaxies is thought to be two million light-years. There do not appear to be any stars outside the galaxies, just as there are no towns or villages in the ocean. Even though the billions of glittering stars in a galaxy appear as clouds, the universe is so vast that each star moves through space like a lone Arab walking across sandy stretches of the Sahara Desert.

"Now, what's the point I am making?" asks John Glenn. He replies that he is trying to make evident the orderliness of the whole universe about us from the smallest atomic structure to the greatest thing we can visualize: galaxies millions of light-years distant in space, all traveling in exact prescribed orbits in relation to one another.

"Could all this have just happened?" Glenn asks. "Was this an accident? Someone tossed up a bunch of flotsam and jetsam, and it suddenly started making these orbits all of its own accord? I can't believe that's really true. I think this was a definite plan. This is one big thing in space that shows me there is a God. It wasn't just an accident.

"Let's go on," says John Glenn, "to compare some of our Project Mercury speeds to some of these things we've been talking about. We get to thinking that we're pretty good in this project and that we're really going out with tremendous speeds. But when you think about the tremendous areas of space and speed, our efforts from earth here really are pretty puny."

It was 9:47 A.M. Eastern time, Tuesday, February 20, 1962, when John Glenn blasted off from Cape Canaveral, Florida, atop a giant Atlas rocket. Fifteen minutes later his Mercury space capsule, *Friendship 7*, was soaring over the Canary Islands in the eastern Atlantic. Thus, in a quarter of an hour, Colonel Glenn had covered a distance that had taken Christopher Columbus one month and six days on his first voyage in 1492.

Each full orbiting of the earth took eighty-eight and a half minutes. As he neared the end of his third orbit, Glenn slowed his ship down by firing retro-rockets. The final four miles were a slow descent by parachute. This stretched Glenn's total time to four hours and fifty-six minutes.

Even though Glenn reached a top speed of 17,545 miles per hour, this was far below the speed required for a spacecraft to break the bonds of gravity and head out into space.

A velocity of seven miles per second or about twenty-five thousand miles per hour is needed to escape the gravity pull of the earth. This is known as escape velocity.

If you had a spacecraft that could travel in a straight line from the earth to any of the planets, and if you could maintain a constant speed of twenty-five thousand miles per hour, it would take you about fifty-eight days to reach Mars when it is closest to Earth.

To reach the giant planet Jupiter, you would have to travel in your spacecraft for a year and nine months. If you wished to visit triple-ringed Saturn, you would have to travel three and a half years. To reach tiny Pluto, the last planet of the solar system, would take you sixteen years!

And these are merely the planets. To reach the nearest star visible in the night sky, Alpha Centauri, would take you more than *a hundred thousand years*!

By contrast, it takes a beam of light only five and a half hours to reach Pluto, and four and a half years to touch down at Alpha Centauri.

Light from some of the outlying stars is thousands upon thousands of years old. Some stars are so distant that by the time the light reaches you the stars themselves may no longer be in existence. They may be burned out and cold as cinders.

Our sun is but one of some two hundred billion stars arranged in space like a huge wagon wheel or dinner plate. We call this island of stars the Milky Way galaxy. Our sun and planet are located near the outside of this wheel. Hence, when we look up we see stars so distant they appear as a hazy white band encircling the entire sky. This broad, faint band of light extends like a veil across the vastness of space. It may remind you of a road or lane across the heavens, and this is exactly what the ancients thought it to be: a milk-white road — the Milky Way.

In 1924, Edwin P. Hubble, working with the new 100-inch telescope on Mount Wilson, discovered the first galaxy outside our own Milky Way, the Andromeda galaxy. Since then, thousands upon thousands of other galaxies have been discovered, each an island universe in itself.

And the amazing thing is that while our earth is circling around our sun at the rate of sixty-five thousand miles per hour, and our sun is circling around our galaxy, the galaxies themselves are running away from each other at the cosmic speed of twenty-five thousand miles per second.

No wonder John Glenn said of Project Mercury, "Thinking in terms of what's already going on in space, this is really a pretty puny human effort."

Soviet cosmonaut Gherman Titov said that during his orbit around the world he looked out into space but did not see God.

"You can't measure God in that way," said John Glenn. "We can't see, feel, smell or touch our religious power. It's an intangible something."

The same thing is true, John Glenn goes on to say, if we are getting ready to test a new airplane. It may have the most powerful engine in the world. It can have the finest aerodynamic design. It may go the fastest. But for the airplane to fulfill its mission, what do we have to do? We have to give it direction. And how do we do this? We do this by reference to our compass in the airplane. Now the force that runs the compass you can't see, feel, touch, taste, smell. It defies all of our senses. We know it's there because we see the results.

Pilots have staked their lives literally thousands of times, trusting that the compass will give the proper reading and will guide them where they should go.

"The same is true of the Christian principles in our lives," says John Glenn. "We see the results. We know they are there. There's no doubt about it."

At his request, Glenn was released from his assignment to NASA in 1964. He wanted to retire from the Marine Corps in order to enter the Ohio Democratic senatorial race. He was grounded, however, when he fell in his home and sustained damage to his inner ear. John Glenn eventually prevailed and was elected to office in 1974.

In his office on Capitol Hill, a reporter asked Senator Glenn: "After *Friendship 7* you said, in regard to achievement in space, that we have 'only scratched the surface.' Have we penetrated the surface yet?"

"No," replied Glenn. "In fact, I am more impressed with how little we know than with how much we know. Ever since the caveman looked over the hill to the next valley, man has realized there is so much more to learn, to question, to examine. Even with all our accomplishments through space research, we have just barely scratched the surface."

It is interesting to note how John Glenn's comments on space and the universe reflect those of Dr. Wernher von Braun. "Anything as well ordered and perfectly created as is our earth and universe," said von Braun, "must have a Maker, a Master Designer. Anything so orderly, so perfect, so precisely balanced, so majestic as this creation can only be the product of a Divine Idea. There must be a Maker; there can be no other way."

John Glenn's sentiments also echoed those expressed

by the late Pope Pius XII. During an audience granted to astronomers, Pope Pius said, "Happy is he who can read in the stars the message which they contain, a message worthy of its Author and capable of rewarding the seeker for his tenacity and ability, but inviting him to recognize Him who gives truth and life and who establishes His dwelling in the hearts of those who adore and love Him."

Abraham Lincoln, watching the universe of stars marching in order and precision, remarked: "I can see how it might be possible for a man to look down into the mud and be an atheist, but I cannot conceive how he could look up into the heavens and say there is no God."

"From ancient times," says John Cardinal Wright, "the contemplation of the stars has led men to speculation about God.

"The new age of science," continues Cardinal Wright, "gazing out into God's clear space, may let fresh air into modern thought. These new directions in science may easily recapture the moods of mingled joy and reverence in which the Psalmist wrote: 'I behold your heavens, the work of your fingers, the moon and the stars which you set in place. . . .' "

Cardinal Wright goes on to remind us that, in the new age of space, it is inevitable that religion and science should be kindred forces. If a believer's reaction to the breakthroughs of modern science is truly religious, it will be enthusiastic. The enthusiasm will have its roots in delight at the satisfaction of intellectual curiosity about the universe in which we live. It will also find spiritual joy in the increased insight that scientific discoveries give into the omnipotence, majesty, and wonder of God.

Tonight when you look up at the stars, you are in touch with the universe. You are standing on the edge of vastness. You are standing on the shores of space. Softly as a tremulous dream comes a beam of starlight woven of a thousand yesterdays to speak to you of Him who said: "Let there be lights made in the firmament of heaven, to divide the day and the night, and let them be for signs, and for seasons, and for days, and years."

Each day the pageant of the universe unfolds around you. At dawn God writes His signature upon the mountaintops, and seals it with the gold of morning sun. High on a fortress peak, dark shadows clasp the bright red Indian robes of twilight and fold them in a crevice of the night.

You can catch a glimpse of the beauty of God's kingdom in the crimson end of day's declining splendor when the wizard moon ascends the heavens. With warm importunate hands, the gypsy moon looses night's jewelled scarf and flings its loveliness across the sky. Caressingly he brushes back the twilight's cloud-soft hair and leaves a gentle kiss upon her brow.

At this hour of enchantment, all creation praises God, singing of His beauty, and entreating His benediction for the night. At this time the heart kneels — and did all men with one accord kneel too, the kingdom of God would, without hindrance and without delay, be established on this earth.

Flung in generous handfuls across the velvet black of night are gems dazzling beyond even Sinbad's most fabulous dreams. There is bright Algol, beloved of camel drivers, and blue Deneb, golden Dubhe, and Vega, the pale sapphire. Mighty Rigel blazes bluish-white, a jewel made for a king! Betelgeuse glows moody as an opal, while lovely Aldebaran blossoms like a pale ruby in the distant sky.

That golden blur of light shimmering just south of overhead is the Pleiades, "the Seven Sisters of Heaven," sending forth a soft, sweet radiance. Many a night you may have seen the Pleiades rising through the mellow shade, then glitter like a swarm of fireflies caught in a silver braid.

From rim to rim across the bowl of the sky, glimmers the star-studded haze called the Milky Way, that ribbon of light woven of flaming suns. The poet tells us:

The sky is a dark drinking cup
That was overturned of old,
And it pours in the eyes of men
Its wine of airy gold.

We drink that wine all day,
Till the last drop is drained up,
And we are lighted off to bed
By the jewels in the cup.

The drinking cup of the heavens is the Big Dipper. Its stars on the lip side point to that compass in the sky, the North Star.

Ancient peoples of southern Europe as well as our own Indians had a different name for the Big Dipper. They called it the Great Bear. The three stars in the Big Dipper's long handle were the tail of the Great Bear!

The shimmering magic of the midnight sky is caught in Henry Wadsworth Longfellow's immortal "Hymn to the Night":

I heard the trailing garments of the Night
  Sweep through her marble halls!
I saw her sable skirts all fringed with light
  From the celestial walls!

I felt her presence by its spell of might,
  Stoop o'er me from above;
The calm, majestic presence of the Night,
  As of the one I love.

The nightly pageant of the stars has thrilled and comforted the heart of man through many long centuries. From the plains of ancient Israel, David, king of song, looked up at the stars and sang of them on his harp. St. Joseph, man of prayer, saw the great stars leap to their vigils the night he took Mary and the Child and fled into Egypt.

Columbus, builder of dreams, looked up from the swirling waters of the vast Atlantic and saw the familiar stars of the Big Dipper. With their assurance came the calm command, "Sail on."

As you watch the bright stars flaming high over the rooftops, they repeat for you their story. They tell you of Him whose power balances their ponderous weights and keeps them spinning in the harmony of their circles. Suddenly you realize the truth uttered by the Royal Psalmist: "The heavens declare the glory of God, and the firmament proclaims his handiwork."

And in the quiet of the moment you slip close to God, having come to Him by the stairway of the stars.

14 13 12 11 10 9
8 7 **6** 5 4 3 2 1

FIRST PRAYER AT
17,544 MPH

The spirit of faith and prayer that marked the space age was evident when astronaut Gordon Cooper circled the earth in May of 1963. He had named his Mercury spacecraft *Faith 7* because of his belief in God. The thirty-six-year-old air force major traveled in an orbit that varied from 100.2 to 165.8 miles. Due to the speed of his spacecraft — some 17,544 miles per hour — his "nights" were less than forty-five minutes long.

During his third orbit of the earth, Cooper conducted an interesting experiment. He released a sphere that contained a flashing beacon of light. The sphere went into an orbit slightly beneath Cooper's and he was unable to see the beacon at first.

However, on the fourth orbit, while approaching Hawaii on the dark side of the earth, he saw the sun reflecting on the sphere. Once he had spotted it, Cooper could distinguish its flashing lights. There were two sixty-thousand-watt xenon lights on the sphere.

The press kit commemorating NASA's twentieth anniversary informs us that in 1963 astronaut Gordon Cooper set the U.S. record for the longest manned mission to date. He completed twenty-two orbits in thirty-four hours and twenty minutes.

During his seventeenth orbit around planet Earth, deep in the darkness of the night, high over the Indian Ocean, Cooper composed a prayer, which he placed on a tape recorder. This recorded prayer was played back to the Congress of the United States, and later broadcast to the nation.

In this prayer Gordon gave thanks to God for the privilege of soaring through the splendid realms of space and of being able to look down on the fascinating globe we call planet Earth. He concluded his prayer with a request for God to continue to stretch out His hand in loving protection over all of us.

I sometimes wonder what would happen if our prayers were put on a tape recorder. Would they sound like Gordon Cooper's, or would they sound more like the following one, reported to have been composed by an unknown businessman in London in the last century:

> O Lord, Thou knowest that I have nine houses in the City of London and likewise that I have lately purchased an estate in fee simple in the County of Essex. Lord, I beseech Thee to preserve the Counties of Essex and Middlesex from fires and earthquakes; and as I have a mortgage in Hertfordshire, I beg Thee likewise to have an eye of compassion on that county. And, Lord, for the rest of the counties, Thou mayest deal with them as Thou art pleased.
>
> O Lord, enable the bank to answer all their bills, and make all my debtors good men. Give a prosperous voyage and return to the Mermaid sloop, which I have insured, and Lord, Thou hast said, that 'the days of the wicked are short,' and I trust Thou wilt not forget Thy promises, having purchased an estate in revirsion of Sir. J. P., a profligate young man.
>
> Sanctify, O Lord, this night to me by preserving me from thieves and fire and make my servant honest and careful while I Thy servant lie down in Thee, O Lord. Amen.

FIRST AMERICAN
SPACE WALK

Who is the most popular fantasy hero?

Is it Luke Skywalker or Princess Leia of *Star Wars*, or someone from *Battlestar Galactica*?

Judged by the length of time he has been popular, perhaps the honor should go to Superman. The story line for *Superman* was laid out in Jerry Siegel and Joe Schuster's comic books some forty years ago.

Since 1955 *Superman* has appeared continuously on TV in every major city of the United States and in almost every foreign country except those under Communist rule. In Japan, Hirohito declared the *Superman* TV show, with dubbed-in Nipponese dialogue, his favorite series.

In December 1978 *Superman* was released as the big Christmas movie of the season. In the film, Superman not only flies better and faster than any bird or plane, but he does aerial acrobatics that would cause an eagle to fasten its seat belt. Perhaps here, indeed, is the reason for the appeal of Superman. Ever since the dawn of creation, man has desired to fly through the air with the greatest of ease.

Over seventy years ago in London a new play, *Peter Pan*, was produced on the stage. In one scene, the audience is told that anybody can fly if he wishes hard enough.

At the matinee performances, several children leaped

out of their balcony seats, eyes shut, wishing hard — and landed in the hospital. At subsequent performances it was announced that a special "fairy dust" had to be sprinkled on your shoulders first, and the casualties ceased.

Our first astronaut to imitate, at least to some extent, the agility of Peter Pan and Superman was astronaut Edward H. White. The facts of his flight are given in calm, detached language in NASA's twentieth-anniversary press kit: "June 3, 1965, *Gemini 4* spacecraft, with astronauts James A. McDivitt and Edward H. White as pilots, launched to make sixty-two revolutions around the earth in ninety-seven hours and fifty-six minutes, during which White became the first American to walk in space."

What a thrill it must have been for Edward White when he stepped out of the *Gemini* and found himself alone in space and master of all he surveyed.

Perhaps he felt as though he were waltzing with the stars in his eyes, the moon at his elbow, and the earth spread out beneath him like a giant balloon made by God for His children to enjoy.

Although White was speeding at 17,500 miles per hour, there was no wind blowing against him, nothing tugging on his space suit. In the near-vacuum of space he moved silently and swiftly — a modern-day Peter Pan or Superman leaping through God's glorious kingdom.

During these thrilling moments it must have seemed to Edward White that he had slipped the surly bonds of earth and climbed towards the sun to become a modern-day Icarus. High in the sunlit silence he wheeled and soared and swung, and did a hundred things we earth-bound mortals only dream of.

White looked down on the blue Pacific a hundred and twenty miles below and noticed that he was approaching the coast of California. At this moment, from inside the cockpit of the *Gemini*, Jim McDivitt pointed a camera straight down to catch White orbiting as a human satellite, while far beneath him the wrinkled ocean crawled.

Perhaps the nearest thing that people do today to taste something of the delight that Edward White experienced is to take up the sport of skydiving.

A sky diver's delight is to bail out of a plane for a mile-high free-fall. As he plunges earthward in a long, controlled dive for thousands of feet before opening the lifesaving canopy, the sky diver experiences a special kind of communion with infinity. You may call it "the rapture of the blue." Some refer to it as "the fine art of falling."

Men and women who fall for thrills are infected with a virus that leaves them forever craving for longer and longer free-falls. Like fledgling eagles, they wish to soar in the wild, blue yonder. As they crouch by the open door of the plane waiting to drop, they are caught up by the song of wanderlust. The framework and struts of the plane hum and chord like a harp. The wind brushes over their ears with bright feathers of sound.

You and I think of a parachute as an emergency device — an escape mechanism from a point of no return. Sky divers think of chutes as necessary impediments to long free-falls. Their primary interest is in a true detachment from earth.

Edward White admitted that he was so taken up by the "rapture of the blue" that he was reluctant to climb back into the spacecraft.

When White finally sat down alongside James McDivitt inside the *Gemini 4*, the two astronauts started to close the hatch. To his horror, White discovered that the hatch had a malfunction. The closing lever was turning free without ratcheting the hatch down. At this moment, monitors at mission control in Houston saw his pulse hit 178.

While McDivitt pulled hard on a lanyard attached to the hatch, White used one hand to press down a spring and the other to turn the ratchet lever. The hatch was finally sealed and the cabin could be repressurized.

Concerning this ordeal, White later said that their

Astronaut James A. McDivitt, who orbited the earth sixty-two times aboard Gemini 4 *with Edward H. White.* (NASA *photo*)

good luck in finally closing the hatch was not the result of any strength of their own: "It was that the faith we had in our training, in each other, and in our God didn't leave room for negative thoughts."

Although the *Gemini 4* splashed down fifty-six miles short of the carrier, navy divers from helicopters were alongside within ten minutes after touchdown. McDivitt was the first to climb out of the hatch and jump into the life raft. Fifty-five minutes after touchdown, the two astronauts were delivered to the *Wasp* by helicopter, in need of a shave and shower.

Because of their cramped positions in the spacecraft, doctors thought that both McDivitt and White would suffer from the same effects that befall bedridden people who attempt to get up suddenly. Too much blood may pool in the calves and feet with not enough reaching the brain. The result can be a blackout. Soviet doctors reported that some cosmonauts suffered such cardiovascular effects for seven to ten days after flights.

Fortunately, McDivitt and White were remarkably free of such effects, though they did show some signs of hypotension.

While McDivitt and White were getting their first good night's sleep on the carrier, NASA was developing its color film. These films and photographs opened up space to the popular imagination more dramatically than ever. The most dramatic photo was one taken one hundred miles up in space. As White floated in front of McDivitt's hatch window, the command pilot took an incredibly sharply defined photo with his 70-mm Hasselblad camera. White is shown floating directly in front of McDivitt's hatch, each star crisp in the small U.S. flag on his shoulder, and the cylindrical *Gemini 4* itself eerily reflected in his gold-coated protective visor.

One of the amazing things about the flight is that the astronauts themselves were surprised to find out how clearly they could make out earth features. White said that he could make out much greater detail than he could when flying an aircraft at forty thousand feet. He was delighted to discover that he could even make out roads and the wakes of ships clearly.

After the astronauts returned to the United States, a reporter asked Edward H. White whether or not he had taken along any personal items on the mission. White answered that he had taken along three personal objects. He said that these objects were very important to him because they reflected his attitude and philosophy.

The three objects were: a St. Christopher medal, a gold cross, and a Star of David. These objects were chosen to express his faith in God, his faith in Jim, his faith in the people and in the equipment being used for the mission, and his faith in himself.

Edward White was most emphatic in stating, "Faith was the most important thing I had going for me on the flight." Since it was impossible to take something representing every religion in the country, White said he took the three with which he was most familiar.

He then went on to say that he was "absolutely amazed" at the beautiful reaction that took place across America when people learned that he had taken the St. Christopher medal, the gold cross, and the Star of David into space.

People all over the country wrote to Ed White, asking him to explain still more his outlook on religion. What amazed White most of all is that so many of these requests for more information on his religion came from young people. They often expressed surprise that an astronaut could be so interested in the things of God.

White replied that when he was a boy his interest in religion was no greater than that of most young people. His consuming interests were football, track, and camping in the woods.

One great advantage Ed White did have — parents who knew how to communicate their religious beliefs in terms that could be understood and appreciated by a young person. There was never any doubt as to where his parents stood in regard to the importance of religion.

In the White household a Bible was not a decoration or mere conversation piece. It was a book to use. Church-going was not something limited to Christmas and Easter. Going to church every Sunday was as much a part of the weekly calendar as washing clothes on Monday.

Ed's mother knew that the best way to communicate her faith was not through words alone but through her daily actions. She gave a superb demonstration of her confidence in God when Ed's dad, an experienced aviator in the army and the air force, was in a serious accident. Ed was only a young boy when his father took off in a plane from Wright-Patterson Air Force Base. The plane's engines died just after takeoff, and the plane crashed. Ed's father barely survived. It wasn't until years later that Ed learned the extent of his father's injuries.

What impressed Ed most about the experience was the calm, quiet manner in which his mother accepted the tragedy. When his mother finally told the children what a close call their dad had, she listed prayer as the main ingredient that helped save his life.

Ed's dad, like his mother, did most of his communication through action rather than through words. When he was assigned to a base located twelve miles from the crowded, sprawling city of Tokyo, he noticed that the chapel was a dreary, cramped, little quonset hut, more fit for mice than men. One of the first things Ed's dad did was to cooperate with the chaplain in making the chapel as attractive as possible.

The best way to instruct his children about God, according to Ed's dad, was to talk to them in terms of day-to-day experiences. One of his favorite verses from the Bible was, "Ask, and you will receive. Seek, and you will find. Knock, and it will be opened to you."

Ed's dad delighted in illustrating the power of this

verse by recalling times he had asked and then received. The thing he wanted more than anything else when he was a young boy was to receive an appointment to West Point. To everyone's surprise, he got the appointment on his own initiative. When he was sixteen years old he went directly to the most influential man he knew — the editor of the *Sentinel* in Fort Wayne, Indiana. The editor was so impressed by the bright, ambitious young man that he helped him win the appointment.

As the children grew older, Ed's dad emphasized the fact that prayer is not like a bubble gum machine in which you drop a penny and are rewarded with a brightly colored sphere of gum. Faith is not a magic wand you can wave over your head to banish all your troubles and put your feet on easy street. There are times when heaven seems zippered shut. There is no "hot line" open for you to contact God. Instead, you have to patiently plod through the mists that swirl around you on all sides. You are lost in encircling gloom.

Ed first dreamed of becoming an astronaut in 1957, the year that the Russians put *Sputnik* in the sky. At that time Ed had finished West Point and was stationed in Germany. Although Ed's feet were anchored on planet Earth, his dreams were soaring through space — all the way to the moon.

Alas, Ed was not qualified, and so began the long climb up the mountain of learning which would lead him to his dreams. He enrolled in the University of Michigan. It was while there that Ed met Jim McDivitt and was delighted to learn that Jim shared his dream of spaceflight.

Following graduation from the university, Ed became a test pilot at Wright-Patterson Air Force Base, Ohio. While there Ed had an opportunity to apply to NASA for the manned-spaceflight program. To his overwhelming delight, he was selected.

Ed's dream was coming closer. He moved with his wife, Pat, and his children, Eddie and Bonnie, to the

Manned Spacecraft Center in Houston, where he bought a home.

Imagine Ed's surprise when he and the other men in the space program received a very special gift from Pope John XXIII — a medal of St. Christopher, the patron saint of travelers.

The choice of materials to take along on a trip in space is not an easy one. Materials have to space-qualify. Certain materials will outgas — give off gases due to the extremes of pressure and temperature encountered in space. They might even dissolve. Since gold is a "noble" or inactive metal, it qualifies; hence, Ed's first thought was to take along a small gold cross as a symbol of his faith. Then his glance fell on the medal given to him by Pope John. Why not take this medal along too? And why not include a Star of David?

The next morning during breakfast, when Ed explained the ideas to his wife, Pat, she was ecstatic. Immediately Pat suggested to Ed that he take along her own gold cross. Unfortunately, her cross was too small; so, while her husband was making the final preparations for the flight, Pat hurried out and purchased a gold cross and a gold Star of David.

Ed wrapped all three items in two small flags: an American flag to indicate that we here in the United States live in brotherhood, and a United Nations flag to indicate the hope that someday all the people of planet Earth will live in brotherhood.

It was June 3, 1965, when Jim McDivitt and Ed White arrived at Launchpad 19 on Cape Kennedy. Ed was carrying the three symbols sewn into a special pouch on the left leg of his space suit.

Ed was quite fascinated to learn that Jim had brought along his own St. Christopher medal, which he fastened to his instrument panel. Once the *Gemini 4* was in orbit, and everything in the spacecraft was weightless, the medal floated lazily on the end of its short chain, a sparkling reminder to Ed and Jim of the fact that Pope John was praying for them — as were millions of fellow Americans.

When Ed returned home after the *Gemini 4* flight, his children were most eager to see the symbols. Bonnie, age nine, and Eddie, age eleven, wanted to find out whether or not the trip through space had changed the three items.

One of the best possible uses to which these tokens can be put, according to Ed, is that whenever we are asked questions concerning the significance of the medal and the crosses, we can make use of this golden opportunity to inform people of the presence of God in our lives.

The father of astronaut Edward H. White II is a retired air force major general. Following the death of his astronaut son, Major General Edward H. White penned a beautiful letter to his grandson to remind him that no one knows better than an astronaut just how important faith is. When an astronaut steps out of a spacecraft speeding at 17,500 miles per hour far above planet Earth, he has to have faith — faith in his equipment, in the knowledge and skill of hundreds of other men, in his own endurance and training; and, above all, faith in God into whose hands he commits himself whether things go well or badly.

The general concluded his letter by mentioning that his son, Ed, was of the opinion that it is our destiny as children of God to keep seeking new challenges, asking new questions, finding new answers. The farther into space we probe, the more mysteries we will encounter. All this will be additional proof of the infinite power and wisdom and beauty of God.

Astronaut James A. McDivitt, who orbited the earth sixty-two times with Edward H. White II aboard *Gemini 4*, was born June 10, 1929, in Chicago. He received his early schooling at St. Philomena and St. Mel parishes on Chicago's West Side.

On the day of his historic takeoff for the sixty-two-orbit adventure in space, McDivitt received Holy Communion in his quarters at 4:45 A.M. on June 3, 1965.

71

One day after his return from space, astronaut McDivitt was addressing members of the Foreign Press Club in Rome. "I did not see God looking into my space-cabin window," said McDivitt, "as I do not see God looking into my car's windshield on earth. But I could recognize His work in the stars as well as when walking among flowers in a garden. If you can be with God on earth, you can be with God in space as well."

The spirit of faith and prayer manifested by astronauts James McDivitt and Edward White is symbolized beautifully in the memorial window of the Strategic Air Command Memorial Chapel. I saw this window on Saturday, November 25, 1978, when I was invited to a tour of the Offutt Air Force Base south of Omaha, Nebraska.

When I entered the chapel, I was so overcome by the beauty of this glorious window that all I could do was to stand and feast my eyes.

If I could use words for brush strokes to paint you a picture of this inspiring window, I'd do so. Lacking that, all I can do is to offer you the description given in the leaflet I was given.

"Most prominent in the design is the ray of golden light symbolic of God, His will, His revelation, and His influence on the life of man. Standing in the fullness of God's will is man [pictured as a pilot]. He is responding to the challenge of God to serve his age. . . . Mature in mind and dedicated in spirit, he stands upon the threshold of the unknown in response to the challenge of God. . . ."

FIRST MAN TO 'WALK' AROUND THE PLANET

On Sunday, June 5, 1966, astronaut Eugene Cernan became the first man in history to "walk" completely around planet Earth.

When I inform my students of this fact, they wonder how anyone can walk around the planet. Actually, Eugene Cernan did not walk. When he climbed out of the *Gemini 4* space capsule, he simply continued to move with it at the same speed.

The secret of Cernan's walk is a combination of two things — centrifugal force and gravity. This same secret applies to all spacecraft in orbit.

If you took physics in high school, you may remember that "any body in motion will continue its motion in a straight line unless compelled by external forces to do otherwise." This is Newton's first law of motion: It is the explanation of centrifugal force.

Centrifugal force is always trying to make things flee their center of rotation. When David let the stone fly from his sling, it shot away like a mad bumblebee with disaster buzzing in its bonnet. It was a forceful demonstration of centrifugal force that brought down Goliath.

Eugene Cernan, the man who "walked" around planet Earth, was also mission commander for Apollo 17, the sixth and final manned lunar-landing mission in the Apollo program. (NASA photo)

At present we are victims of centrifugal force. Planet Earth is like a giant top spinning in space. So tremendous is this spinning that the equator speeds around in dizzy revolutions of a thousand miles per hour. Along the circle from Panama to Baghdad, the natives clip off some twenty-four thousand miles each day, globe-trotting in one spot. Meanwhile our Eskimo friends at the North Pole simply turn around once on their heels.

This centrifugal motion makes the earth bulge out in the middle like a juicy tomato, with the amazing result that the equator is thirteen and a half miles farther from the center of the earth than are the North and South Poles.

This tomato shape of our earth means that the Mississippi River runs uphill. The same mysterious, fascinating, centrifugal force that causes the ever-spinning earth to bulge at the equator also sends equator-bound waters up the longest hill on earth.

You may wonder why this centrifugal force does not hurl you into space the way that a penny is shot out from the turning record on your record player. (Try placing a penny near the outside rim of a moving turntable and see what happens.)

For the answer, go back in memory to the dewy days of your youth when you tied a bucket of water to a rope and twirled it around your head. You were immediately aware of the pull on the rope.

The reason the bucket did not fall and hit you on the head — even though you were pulling on the rope — is that centrifugal force (center-fleeing force) was trying to make it move outward from the center of rotation. The rope, in turn, kept centrifugal force from running away with the bucket of water.

If the rope had broken, you could then no longer have counterbalanced the centrifugal force. The pull towards the center would have been gone, and the bucket would have taken off in a straight line — spacebound for anywhere.

We are held to the surface of the earth by the rope of gravity. If the earth were to spin seventeen times faster than it does at present, you would never dare travel to Panama. Gravity could not counterbalance the additional outward thrust of centrifugal force. You would be hurled out into space.

Now let's apply all this to Eugene Cernan. Left to himself, Cernan's forward speed of eighteen thousand miles per hour would carry him five miles straight forward in one second. During the same second, however, gravity pulled Cernan and his capsule sixteen feet toward the center of the earth. (Cernan and his capsule were like the bucket of water trying to move forward. Gravity was the invisible rope pulling them to the center.)

The result — Cernan and his capsule acted like the bucket of water: They moved in a circle.

It may all seem rather simple, but consider the dangers. If the rope on your bucket of water is not strong enough, the rope will break. If Cernan's forward speed became too great, gravity could no longer hold him, and he would sail away into space to vanish forever.

You may recall what happened when you did not turn your bucket of water fast enough. Gravity pulled it down to the ground. Again, the same thing applied to Cernan and his space capsule. If its forward speed had not been able to balance the pull of gravity, it would have fallen from the sky.

No wonder that Eugene Cernan was only too well aware of the fact that every second of his life depended on God. His parents, too, were alert to the fact. The morning of their son's space walk, Mr. and Mrs. Andrew Cernan attended early Mass at St. Simeon's Church in Bellwood, Illinois.

Three weeks after his historic space walk the people of Eugene Cernan's hometown turned out a hundred and fifty thousand strong for a two-mile parade and a roaring welcome.

Since Eugene Cernan had walked through God's great realms of space, it was only fitting that he begin the special day set aside in his honor by attending Mass to thank the great God of Space for His protection during the space walk. In company with his family, parents, and relatives, Cernan attended the 8:30 A.M. Mass at St. Simeon's Church.

Thus, by his public actions, Eugene Cernan gave proof of the spirit of faith and prayer that has been the hallmark of our men of the space age.

Eugene Cernan took off for space again on May 18, 1969, in the *Apollo 10*, which was launched as a dress rehearsal for the moon landing. The mission lasted eight days and three minutes. And Cernan made public the fact that he prayed during the final moon orbit.

Every now and then newspapers give a lot of publicity to men who pray in public. I recall the forceful, dramatic photo of the Pittsburgh Steelers with their owner, Art Rooney, kneeling in prayer to give thanks to God for winning Super Bowl IX in New Orleans, defeating the Minnesota Vikings, 16-6. The Steelers were most grateful to the Almighty for winning their first National Football League championship in forty-two years.

There was no newspaperman with camera to capture Eugene Cernan when he made the Sign of the Cross and prayed. In their final orbit around the moon, during the crucial moments that preceded the firing of the rocket engine that would begin their return to planet Earth, all three *Apollo 10* astronauts turned to God in prayer.

Sometimes my students remark that they are confused by a seeming repetition of events in our space history. Did not Eugene Cernan, for example, merely repeat what Ed White had done before him?

The answer is a confusing yes and no.

Both astronauts, for example, went through the same physical act of crawling out of their space capsules to walk in space.

There is, however, this difference. Edward White *was* the first American to walk in space! But he was outside his space capsule for only twenty minutes when he was told by the flight director in Houston to get back into the *Gemini 4*. This was America's first EVA (extravehicular activity) and NASA wanted to proceed with caution. White's walk was really a test for both man and equipment.

Although White's space walk looked easy, it was a gamble that could have ended disastrously. Once he left the protective walls of the *Gemini 4*, White's life depended entirely upon the effectiveness of his space suit and the gear he carried, heretofore tested only in conditions of simulated space. To subdue the searing glare of the sun, his helmet was shaded by a tinted outer visor. With ten extra layers of material added to it, his suit shielded him from incredible extremes of temperature of +250 F on sunlit surfaces to -150 F on the shady sides. The suit was also designed to protect him from deadly cosmic radiation and from possible bombardment by micrometeorites that zip through space at speeds hundreds of times faster than high-velocity rifle bullets. One puncture in the pressurized suit would have set his blood to boiling within seconds and made him explode like a toy balloon.

One year after Edward White had walked in space some hundred and twenty miles above the Pacific, NASA was so confident of its equipment it allowed Eugene Cernan to become the first and only man in space to walk *completely* around planet Earth.

Another item that may be confusing is this. Some astronauts went on more than one mission in space; hence, their names are linked to different chapters in space history. Astronaut John Young made four space missions.

Two of astronaut James Lovell's four space trips were to the moon. He was on the historic Christmas Eve lunar orbit in 1968. In 1970 he narrowly escaped with his life on *Apollo 13*.

Eugene Cernan, in addition to being the first and only

man to walk completely around planet Earth, was also mission commander for *Apollo 17*, the sixth and final manned lunar-landing mission in the Apollo program. The last footprint left on the cold surface of the moon was that of Eugene Cernan.

14 13 12 11 10 9
8 7 6 5 4 3 2 1

FIRST PRAYER
ABOVE THE MOON

The most exciting Christmas Eve I ever experienced was in 1968. I could hardly believe my ears when I sat by my radio and listened to the voices of men coming from the moon as they took turns reading the first page of the Bible. And then, the first prayer ever uttered by a human being above the surface of the moon. It was a Christmas Eve to recall forever as a dynamic expression of the faith and prayer of our astronauts.

I was not the only one glued to the radio on that Christmas Eve. It is estimated that one out of every four persons on earth, nearly a billion people in sixty-four countries, heard the story of creation as the *Apollo 8* astronauts read the Bible.

The log of *Apollo 8* began at 7:51 A.M. on December 21 with the lift-off from the Kennedy Space Center. The 363-foot-tall rocket with no fewer than three and a half million working parts performed flawlessly. The astronauts left earth's orbit on their six-day journey at 24,200 miles per hour, just 429 miles slower than the speed at which they returned to earth. It was a smooth TLI (translunar injection), but then something developed to remind the men in space that they were still mortals. Astronaut James Lovell informed Mission Control Center in Houston that Borman

80

had been sick for some hours with a virus that caused nausea, headache, and vomiting. Astronauts Lovell and Anders were not feeling too chipper either.

To counter the attack of what was thought to be twenty-four-hour flu, the crewmen took Lomotil. Fortunately, by the time the astronauts were some 138,700 miles from earth, they had recovered.

On the afternoon of December 23, when the *Apollo 8* spacecraft was 212,000 miles from planet Earth, astronaut Lovell looked through the window of his spaceship and reported that he could see the entire section of the planet from Baja, California, to Cape Horn at the tip of South America.

Lovell thrilled to the colors of his hometown planet. The waters had a tint of royal blue. Clouds were white and dazzling. Land areas were generally a brownish texture. All the proud works of man vanished: Cities, roads, and bridges were obliterated by distance. The earth hung suspended in the sky as a brilliant, beautiful but mysterious ball. It appeared to be about four times bigger than the moon appears to us on earth.

On Monday afternoon, December 23, the *Apollo 8* reached the equigravisphere — the Great Divide of space 202,700 miles from the earth and 38,900 miles from the moon. This is the place in space where the pull of the earth in one direction is balanced by the pull of the moon in the other direction. After passing this spot in space, the *Apollo 8* entered into the gravitational pull of the moon.

Radio contact with *Apollo* was lost as the ship passed behind the moon out of sight of earth. Not until *Apollo 8* emerged from behind the moon did the world learn that it was in an elliptical orbit ranging between 69 and 195 miles above the moon.

For about twenty hours, a total of ten orbits, *Apollo 8* remained locked in the grip of the moon. During this time the astronauts studied the moon and took an imposing array of still and motion pictures, many of them in color.

Each time astronauts Borman, Lovell, and Anders vanished behind the far side of the moon, they lost all contact with earth for forty-five minutes on each of the ten orbits.

Never before had man traveled so far so fast or looked so closely at another celestial body. Never before had so many millions listened and watched, their imaginations stretched, as the explorers spoke across the emptiness. Never, indeed, had adventure ever borne all mankind so daringly near the boundaries of its aspirations.

As the *Apollo 8* orbited over the naked plains, the barren mountains, and the huge craters of the moon, Lovell reported: "The vast loneliness up here is awe-inspiring, and it makes you realize just what you have back there on earth. The earth from here is a grand oasis in the big vastness of space."

Lovell went on to say that the moon "is essentially gray. No color. Looks like plaster of Paris or sort of a grayish deep sand."

"The back side (of the moon)," said Anders, "looks like a sandpile my kids have been playing in. . . . It's all beat up, no definition, just a lot of bumps and holes."

Anders took special delight in the lunar sunrises and sunsets. "These bring out the stark nature of the terrain," Anders said. "The sky up here is also a rather forbidding, foreboding expanse of blackness. You can see by the numerous craters that this planet [the moon] has been bombarded through the eons with numerous small asteroids and meteoroids pockmarking the surface every square inch."

Describing the moon as vast, lonely and forbidding, astronaut Borman comments that it is "not a very inviting place to live or work."

On Christmas Eve as the *Apollo 8* soared around the moon and the astronauts looked down on planet Earth 240,000 miles away, the first men to circle the moon took turns reading the first ten verses of Genesis, the story of creation.

As *Apollo 8* sped past the craters and mountains of the moon at 3,643 miles per hour, the voices of the three astronauts were heard on radios and television sets around the world. The words of Genesis, recited from what, a generation ago, was considered an unreachable celestial sphere, took on new meaning. In sight as well as sound, earthbound men could gain a new grasp of the miracle of the creation.

The three *Apollo 8* astronauts imparted to the peoples of earth a deeply moving religious experience to accompany their excitement over the stupendous achievement of man's first circling of the moon.

Then Borman said the first prayer ever uttered by man above the surface of the moon: "Give us, O God, the vision which can see Thy love in the world in spite of human failure. Give us the faith to trust Thy goodness in spite of our ignorance and weakness."

This prayer proved so popular it appeared on Christmas cards in 1969. Later it was printed on the covers of monthly missalettes.

The prayer, and the reading from Genesis, had a tremendous impact on people around the earth. As Christmas lights flickered across the globe, people knelt before altars on every continent. Others pondered the miracle of life in their own way. The words of devotion from high above the moon made a deep impression. To some, the voices from the space vehicle named for a Roman deity had the ring of the voice of God Himself.

On Christmas morning, the families of all the astronauts attended church services — the Bormans and Lovells at Episcopalian churches, the Anderses at a Roman Catholic church. Marilyn Lovell wore a new mink coat, a Christmas gift that her husband arranged to have delivered from Neiman-Marcus on Christmas morning. "It came," she said happily, "from the man in the moon."

Borman said that the astronauts had no idea of the tremendous impact their Christmas message had made until, back in Houston, they looked over the stacks of thousands upon thousands of letters (as many as twenty-nine thousand in a single week) sent to them from all over the world.

"The flight was so uncannily perfect from the technical aspect," Borman remarked, "that it almost bordered on miraculous." The three and a half million working parts of the *Apollo 8* performed flawlessly.

Upon his return to planet Earth, astronaut Frank Borman was asked how and when he had decided to read from the Book of Genesis. Borman replied that the decision went back to November 1968, when the three astronauts were informed that, during the TV presentation from the moon on Christmas Eve, they would have probably the largest audience that had ever listened to the human voice. The question that became a preoccupation with Borman was: "What can we do that's special?"

Over the next several evenings Borman telephoned dozens of friends — men whose opinions he respected. He called people at the launch site. He called Washington and telephoned home to ask his wife, Susan, and the two boys for their thoughts.

After much discussion and careful thought, the astronauts decided that perhaps the first ten verses of Genesis might adequately express their emotion.

At first they decided to take along a small Bible. But there was a problem. Bibles are made of flammable material. They would have to be covered with a special fireproof material, and they would be a little difficult to get at. It would be better if the selection were typed right into the flight plan itself. The paper on which this plan of every detail of the flight is printed was made of flame-resistant material. It would be easy to schedule the reading of the creation story into one of their regular telecasts.

And so, into the official record of the first flight of man around the moon went a transcript of the opening ten verses of Genesis.

At 7:01 A.M. on December 21, 1968, the flight began. It was an extraordinarily smooth trip, a brilliant piece of coordinated effort on the part of thousands. "Part of that effort," says Borman, "was prayer. It is astonishing how many people told me they would be praying."

And then the astronauts were at the moon and began their orbit. For about an hour, while they were on the back side of the moon, they were out of contact with earth. Then, when they came around into the light again, there was the earth, seeming to rise up out of darkness. Precisely on schedule, just as planned, the crew took turns reading the ten verses from Genesis.

The prayer that Borman said above the surface of the moon has an equally interesting background. On the Sunday before Borman left his hometown of League City, Texas, to go to Cape Kennedy for the moonshot, he attended St. Christopher's Episcopal Church.

Borman was a lay reader in the Episcopal Church, but had to beg off reading the Scripture lesson at the Christmas Eve service. "You'll do anything to get out of that reading, won't you, Frank," said one of the other lay readers. "Even go to the moon." The lay readers continued to kid Borman about the fact that he wouldn't be around to read on Christmas Eve. Then one of the readers came up with an idea. Wouldn't it be great if Borman could send a message from the moon!

"And so," says Frank Borman, "an idea was planted. I knew that our rector, Father James Buckner, was going to preach that night on the subject of peace. What if we were to send a message — a prayer for peace?"

Rod Rose, a friend of Borman's from the Manned-Spaceflight Center was among those present. He agreed with Borman, and they decided on the first prayer from above the moon.

"Religion is still to me," says Borman, "a very personal thing, and prayer can come at any time of the day or evening. I find it very rewarding."

Borman says that he is not a fundamentalist. He does not believe in a literal interpretation of the Bible. He believes in a liberal interpretation. "Skeptics should remember," says Borman, "it isn't a book of science. I accept its scriptural message — that God created the earth."

In the early part of 1969 Borman made a twenty-day trip through eight countries in Europe and met with the Pope. Upon his return to the States, Borman was asked, "What was the most important reaction of Europeans to your flight and your stated experiences and views?"

In reply, Borman said that he did not speak directly on the subject of religion, yet he found a very fervent response from Europeans to our common desire for peace and brotherhood as stimulated by our first view of our common planet from afar.

The overwhelming impression of the people of Europe was this view that we got of earth. They seemed intensely interested in the fact that there are no barriers and that the success of this mission was due in large measure to contributions made by people the world over.

They responded to the fact that we are really riders on the earth together. And we share such a beautiful planet. It's small and beautiful and fragile.

Borman goes on to say that he is not naive enough to think that things like exploring the moon are going to take away the conflicts that exist on earth, but it helps give us a significant and common point of view.

Earth isn't really very large, Borman reminds us. The atmosphere seems so vast to us here, yet half of it is gone above three miles. To Europeans and Americans both, the overwhelming wonderment is why in the world we can't appreciate what we have.

The miracle of the *Apollo 8* flight to the moon was not the doing of men alone, according to Frank Borman. As he looked down on the bleak, cracked face of the moon, he said he felt as though he were looking at the fingerprints of the Creator.

"I didn't see God," said Borman, "but I saw the evidence that God lives. And through His eyes, that evidence has become clearer to millions the world over."

Apollo 8 astronaut William Anders is a Catholic. Upon his return from the historic spaceflight of December 21-27, 1968, he attended Mass with his wife in Houston.

Speaking of his Christmas over the moon, Anders tells how thrilling it was to look out the spacecraft windows and see our planet floating against the black void of space. "I was amazed," said Anders, "by its delicate beauty. I could clearly see the blue oceans, the greenish-brown lands, and the white clouds swirling below us."

Anders said he knew immediately that this magnificent new vantage point would provide man a tremendously increased capacity to observe and understand the resources of our planet, and, therefore, better enable man to manage it.

"As we coasted out into space," said Anders, "this view diminished in size, and by the time we had reached our lunar rendezvous on Christmas Eve, our earth had become reduced to a tiny, iridescent ball."

Anders reminds us that this was truly a new perspective for mankind from which to view and contemplate his home planet. From the distance of 240,000 miles away, our earth shows up, not as a gigantic and massive place possessed of infinite resources and areas for man to use indiscriminately. Rather, earth is small, finite, and limited — actually, rather puny when compared to the vast blackness through which it drifts. Truly earth is a place which we must learn to handle with more care and understanding.

Anders admits that "This experience had a deep effect on my outlook on life and humanity. If there was one Christmas gift that I wanted to bring back to my family and the world from this lunar expedition, it was this new impression of our home planet. I hoped that I could help man better understand his relationship to nature, his fellowman, and to his God."

Anders feels that this new perspective could help mankind better understand that we are all brothers — riders together on a small planet — that the earth truly belongs to all of us, and that we all must accept the responsibility for its preservation.

"In my opinion," says Anders, "it is quite possible that historians may record that the greatest gain from *Apollo* and space exploration, above all the technical advancements, is this new perspective on mankind and the earth."

Many others agree with Anders that this new perspective and insight from space exploration may, like the Renaissance, help man to see further beyond himself, in order to gain a better understanding of himself and his environment.

Thirty years of teaching convince me of the truth of Anders's statement that, deep in the subconscious, many seem to think of themselves as the center of things, believing that our earth is infinitely large and that problems not immediate to us are far off and do not really exist. Many of us have great difficulty appreciating the existence of our fellowmen on the other side of the globe (and, sometimes, even on the other side of town).

But, after viewing the earth from space and seeing how it really is, the truth is vividly brought home to us: Our earth is a complete entity, and so small compared to the universe.

"One cannot view the earth from space or circle the moon," says Anders, "without experiencing a deep respect for the beauty and orderliness of the universe."

The *Apollo 8* astronauts hope that the birth of the space age will help to begin a new age of understanding for all men. The space age can be a source of inspiration which will offer man both challenges and opportunities to use his unique powers to improve his world and to reaffirm faith in God and the goodness of mankind.

Anders's credo is one we can all repeat. "I believe,"

the astronaut says, "that we are guided in our journey by His wisdom and power, which created this universe, established nature's laws, and set the basis for our faith. I believe that all of us are guided by this same wisdom, power, and faith in our daily lives as we enter this new age of awareness about ourselves.

"I believe our Creator has given man the powers of the human mind and spirit to explore the wonders of this universe so that we can better fulfill His plan. He has endowed man with imagination, curiosity, courage, vision, and dedication, of which space exploration has been a fine example. He has also given us the moral responsibility to use these abilities wisely in order to improve the well-being of all mankind."

According to Anders, the road ahead leads to many wonderful opportunities for all mankind. Our space program is a powerful tool to help us make use of this opportunity. As we progress, the way will be illuminated by the light of knowledge and faith.

When the *Apollo 8* astronauts returned from the moon to planet Earth, I sent each of them a letter of congratulations and a copy of what was then my latest book, now out of print, *Our Romance with Sun and Rain*.

I received this beautiful reply: "Thank you for your well wishes, for your prayers offered in our behalf, and for your congratulations extended on the successful completion of the *Apollo 8*'s historic voyage around the moon.

"We are . . . pleased that we were privileged to participate in man's first interplanetary mission and are most grateful for your kind and generous comments. . . ."

Perhaps the best way to conclude this chapter on man's first Christmas in lunar orbit would be to give you the impression left on the mind of astronaut James Lovell. When he was asked whether or not he could summarize his trip to the moon, James Lovell replied that the experience made him feel as though he had put out his hand and touched the face of God.

FIRST COMMUNION
ON THE MOON

Whether your name is Sally Jo or Moses Maimonides, you will most likely agree that the heavenly body that has had the most influence on man, next to the sun, is the moon.

"God made the two great lights," according to Genesis. "The greater one to govern the day, and the lesser one to govern the night. . . ."

The moon is really a silver-robed messenger from space to speak to us of God's love and care. If He wanted to, God could have left our nights black as a coal hole at midnight without even a glimmer of light from the great beyond. But God is generous and kind. As Robert Louis Stevenson expresses it:

To make this earth, our hermitage,
A cheerful and a pleasant page,
God's bright and intricate device
Of days and seasons doth suffice.

A dash of moonlight seems essential for stories of romance and adventure. It was in a jasmine garden drenched with moonlight that Cyrano De Bergerac stood and called up to Roxane on her balcony, "Your name is like a golden bell hung in my heart; and when I think of you, I tremble, and the bell swings and rings — Roxane! . . . Roxane! . . . along my veins."

Cyrano's cry of love, plangent as the dashing of coastal waters, echoes the fascinating wonder in his heart that transforms the moonlit night into a rhapsody of delight and makes each moment a precious memory, each hour a lifetime.

In his soaring humility, St. Francis claimed the sun as his brother and the moon as his sister. Our sister, the moon, has stood for us through the ages for quiet, mystery, refreshment, and love.

On July 20, 1969, "that orbed maiden with white fire laden, whom mortals call the moon" became our first stepping-stone into space.

It was forty seconds after 3:19 P.M., Sunday afternoon, when the spacecraft officially designated LM (lunar module) 5 — the *Eagle* — landed on the moon.

For the first time in history, man was about to set foot on a heavenly body other than his home planet.

An estimated one sixth of the people on earth listened as a dream of the ages was fulfilled, "Houston, Tranquility Base here. The *Eagle* has landed."

Astronauts Neil A. Armstrong and Edwin E. Aldrin descended to the surface of the moon in the *Apollo 11* lunar module, *Eagle*, while Michael Collins orbited the moon in the command module, *Columbia*.

As Neil Armstrong stepped onto the moon's dusty surface, a message was radioed to millions of anxiously waiting people on earth. "That's one small step for a man," Armstrong said as he stepped onto the lunar soil, "one giant leap for mankind."

There were many scientists as well as astronauts in the NASA program who believed that they were carrying forward God's plan for man in their quest for the moon. They wanted to find the right symbol for the first lunar landing. They wanted to express the feeling that what man was doing in this mission transcended electronics and computers and rockets.

One day when Buzz Aldrin was at Cape Kennedy, working with the sophisticated tools of the space effort, he recalled a sermon by the Rev. Dean Woodruff, pastor of his church, the Webster Presbyterian, just outside Houston. The pastor had mentioned that God frequently reveals Himself in the common elements of everyday life. Traditionally, these elements are bread and wine, common foods in biblical days and typical products of man's labor.

Aldrin wondered whether it might be possible to take Communion on the moon, symbolizing the thought that God was revealing Himself there too, as man reached out into the universe.

As soon as possible, Buzz Aldrin spoke with this pastor about the idea, and the Rev. Dean Woodruff was enthusiastic.

Aldrin told Dean it would be possible to carry the bread in a plastic packet, the way regular in-flight food is wrapped. The wine could also be carried in a plastic container. On the moon there would still be enough gravity for the liquid to pour. Aldrin could drink from a cup or chalice.

Buzz Aldrin asked the pastor to help him find a little chalice which he could take to the moon. The following week, Dean Woodruff showed Aldrin a beautiful silver chalice. Aldrin lifted it, and was pleased to find that it was light enough to take along. Each astronaut is allowed a few personal items on a flight; the wine chalice would be in Aldrin's personal-preference kit.

Pastor Dean Woodruff made plans for two special Communion services at Webster Presbyterian Church. One would be held just prior to Aldrin's leaving Houston for Cape Kennedy. The second would take place on Sunday, July 20, when Neil Armstrong and Buzz Aldrin were scheduled to be on the surface of the moon. On that Sunday, church members back home would gather for Communion while Aldrin joined them, as close as possible to the same hour, taking Communion inside the lunar module.

The first question that came up was whether it would be theologically correct for a layman to serve himself Communion under these circumstances. Pastor Woodruff thought so himself, but to make sure, he decided to write to the stated clerk of the Presbyterian Church's General Assembly.

The answer came back swiftly: "All OK."

The next question was which scriptural passage to use. Which reading would best capture the meaning of this enterprise? Aldrin thought about this a long time, and then selected a passage from the Gospel according to John.

The plan was very simple. Pastor Woodruff would read this same passage to his full congregation at the service back home on earth while Buzz Aldrin was reading it on the moon! If not exactly at the same moment, at least on the same day.

Before Aldrin left Houston for Cape Kennedy, he and his wife, Joan, and their oldest boy, Mike (the only one of the three children of Communion age), went to their church for a special service. There were two loaves on the altar, and two chalices. One of the chalices was the small cup the congregation was giving Buzz to take for the service on the moon.

After the family received Communion, Pastor Woodruff broke off a portion of the second loaf of bread and handed it to Buzz along with the tiny chalice. Within a few hours Buzz was on his way to Cape Kennedy.

The *Saturn 5* rocket that boosted the *Apollo 11* astronauts into space gave them a rough ride at first, but then leveled out for a smooth flight.

On Sunday, July 20, 1969, the astronauts awoke at 5:30 A.M. Houston time. Neil and Buzz separated from Mike Collins in the command module. Their powered descent was right on schedule and perfect except for one un-

Apollo 11 *astronauts Neil A. Armstrong, Michael Collins, and Edwin E. Aldrin.* (NASA photo)

foreseeable difficulty. The automatic guidance system would have taken *Eagle* to an area with huge boulders. Neil had to steer *Eagle* to a more suitable terrain. With only seconds' worth of fuel left, they touched down at forty seconds after 3:18 P.M.

Now Neil and Buzz were sitting inside *Eagle* while Mike circled in lunar orbit, unseen in the black sky above them. In a little while Neil would give the signal to step down the ladder onto the powdery surface of the moon. Now was the moment for the first Communion on the moon.

Buzz Aldrin unstowed the elements from their flight packets. He put them and the Scripture reading on the little table in front of the abort guidance system computer.

Then Buzz called back to Houston. "Houston, this is *Eagle*. This is the LM pilot speaking. I would like to request a few moments of silence. I would like to invite each person listening in, wherever and whoever he may be, to contemplate for a moment the events of the past few hours and to give thanks in his own individual way."

For Aldrin this meant taking Communion. In the radio blackout he opened the little plastic packages which contained bread and wine. He poured the wine into the chalice. In the one-sixth gravity of the moon, the wine curled slowly and gracefully up the side of the cup. It was interesting to think that the very first liquid ever poured on the moon and the first food eaten there were Communion elements.

Just before Aldrin partook of the elements, he read the words which he had chosen to indicate the trust that as man probes into space he is, in fact, acting in Christ.

The first words of Scripture read on the moon were: "I am the vine, you are the branches. He who abides in me, and I in him, he bears much fruit; for without me you can do nothing" (John 15:5).

On that historic Sunday the astronauts placed on the moon a specially prepared capsule containing a dedicatory inscription written personally by Pope Paul VI: "For the glory of the name of God, who gives men such power, we pray and wish well for this wondrous endeavor."

The capsule likewise contained the text of Psalm 8, which Pope Paul had sent the United States government, and which was presented to Dr. Thomas O. Paine, administrator of the National Aeronautics and Space Administration. Psalm 8 is the one which begins: "O Lord, our Lord, how glorious is your name over all the earth. You have exalted your majesty above the heavens."

Four days later, on July 24, the President of the United States stood on the deck of the U.S.S. *Hornet* in mid-Pacific to greet the astronauts who had just returned from a successful mission to the moon.

The President remarked that the millions of people who were following the exploits of the astronauts on TV most likely now felt that their prayers were answered, hence it would be very appropriate if Chaplain Piirto, the chaplain of the *Hornet*, would offer a prayer of thanksgiving.

In his beautiful prayer, Chaplain Piirto mentioned that our minds are staggered and our spirits exultant with the magnitude and precision of the entire *Apollo 11* mission.

"See our enthusiasm," prayed Chaplain Piirto, " and bless our joy with dedicated purpose for the many needs at hand. Link us in friendship with peoples throughout the world as we strive together to better the human condition."

Upon his return to his hometown of Wapakoneta, Ohio, astronaut Neil Armstrong said that he found it difficult to believe anyone could see the sights he was privileged to see and not be most aware of the power of the Supreme Being and His artwork.

One of the most dramatic photos taken during the *Apollo 11* mission is the one taken by the command module pilot, Michael Collins. This photo shows the LM returning to the command module in which Collins had orbited the moon alone while his two companions walked on the moon's surface. What impressed Collins most is the barrenness of the moon's surface.

"As our vehicles probe space," says Collins, "we know for a virtual certainty that our small planet is, in fact, one of a kind. All other environments in the solar system are unimaginably forbidding and hostile.

"It is as if earth were God's grand experiment, a unique garden which He has given us to use and enjoy."

What we did not know until recently, according to Collins, is that our planet, like a lovely garden, is delicate. This discovery began the moment the *Saturn 5* rocket ignited, and the astronauts began to speed away from earth.

On the outbound trip there isn't much time to think about such things. The astronauts were busy looking ahead to the problems of putting the spacecraft into lunar orbit, and then to the lunar landing, and, lastly, to subsequent rendezvous.

Once the lunar module separated from the command module to alight on the moon, astronaut Collins was all by himself, orbiting in the mother ship, *Columbia*, seventy miles above the moon's surface.

Collins could see the rugged, desolate, monotonous surface of the moon clearly. Its endless succession of crevices and fissures have a strange repetitiveness. Collins said he looked in vain for areas identified from earth as the Sea of Nectar, the Sea of Tranquility, the Bay of Dews, the Sea of Cold, and the Lake of Dreams.

Collins saw the moon as a sphere of ghostly distances measured by bleak horizons — a Sahara without an oasis, a Death Valley without a water hole or even a mirage. With savage fierceness the mighty sun strikes the craggy bastions of its soaring mountains and edges them in scarlet. The moon's sun-drenched, sun-glazed hills never know the snow of blossom time nor ever hear thunderbolts crowding upon each other in the valley. Huge craters stare with cyclopean eyes.

Collins found the moon for what it really is. A desert pockmarked with craters, stark and beautiful in its own way, but definitely not a desirable dwelling spot.

Once Collins was rejoined by his companions and they were on their way home, there was time to relax and look out the windows of the space capsule.

We who have never left the earth consider it so big that we find it hard to believe when Collins says, "I looked out my window and tried to find earth. The little planet is so small out there in the vastness that at first I couldn't even locate it. And when I did, a tingling of awe spread over me. There it was, shining like a jewel against the black sky. I looked at it in wonderment, suddenly aware of how its uniqueness is stamped in every atom of my body."

It was at this moment that Collins became aware of his new attitude towards earth. He recalled the days of his youth when he walked along mountain streams and through woods, or stood looking out over fields of corn and wheat. He remembered walking through gardens vibrant with such a splendor of diversity, such richness of color and life. Whether he had walked on concrete sidewalks in the city, or climbed a pathway to a mountain peak, the earth beneath his feet had always seemed solidly anchored.

At that moment in the command module there was a momentary distraction. Collins looked away and . . . poof — earth was gone! "I couldn't find it again," said Collins, "without searching closely."

At this point Collins made still another discovery. He suddenly realized what a tiny, fragile thing our earth is. Such a little gem, such an incredible balance of the universe's rarest ingredients, one that can be ruined all the more easily just because it is so small.

"In that moment," said Collins, "I determined that I would do all I could to let people know what a wonderful home we have — before it is too late.

"So, I have a personal, simple message to pass on: There is only one earth. It is a tiny, precious stone. Let us treasure it; there is not another one."

Upon the return of the *Apollo 11* astronauts from the moon, I sent them a letter of congratulations. In return, they replied: "We are grateful and proud to have participated in the achievement of our national goal of a successful lunar landing and return.

"To those of you who have offered encouragement and good wishes, whose dedicated support has made our programs possible, and whose prayers have sustained us, we extend our humble thanks."

FRONT-PAGE PRAYER

Did you ever see a metropolitan newspaper using the entire front page for an appeal for prayer?

The first and only time I saw such an appeal was on Friday morning, April 17, 1970, when the fate of the *Apollo 13* astronauts was most precarious.

The *Wisconsin State Journal* did something most extraordinary. Using giant-size print they covered the entire front page of the newspaper with this one appeal:

LET US ALL PRAY FOR THEIR SAFE RETURN

Perhaps you may recall the story of man's most perilous week in space when an exploding oxygen tank crippled the *Apollo 13* spacecraft 205,000 miles from planet Earth.

When news flashed from the Houston Space Center that the *Apollo 13* astronauts had turned back from the moon in a crippled ship and might not be able to make it back home, a historic, universal offering of prayer took place around the world. People everywhere began to pray for the safety of the men in space. The Pope offered prayers at St. Peter's, and in almost every country ministers of all religions held prayer services. Men prayed in their homes and at places of work.

Never had there been such a manifestation of human sympathy shown by so many persons of all faiths. They were seeking God's help to bring the three astronauts home safely to their families.

From the moment of the explosion on, the *Apollo 13* pilots steered a very narrow path between life and death. The explosion had blown them off the path which would have taken them around the moon and given them a free return to earth, using the moon's gravity to whip them around and head them back home. Their first move was to try to get back on their course.

Since the explosion had knocked out the engine on their command ship, *Odyssey*, they had to abandon the crippled command ship and crawl into the frail craft *Aquarius*, built to land on the moon.

While the world held its breath, the pilots successfully executed the maneuver, then whipped around the dark side of the moon and headed home.

Two hours after leaving the moon, the astronauts thought they were safely on the narrow corridor necessary to get back to earth. Then another blow. Extensive tracking of *Apollo 13* by ground control showed it was not on a true course and would miss earth by more than a hundred miles, dooming the pilots unless they could correct it.

At 10:31 P.M. on Wednesday, April 15, with another firing of the engine aboard *Aquarius* — which already had done more work than it was ever designed to do — the astronauts put themselves in the corridor for home.

While the pilots labored in space to hold their crippled — and heatless — spaceship together, thousands of engineers and specialists worked feverishly on the ground, devising the new procedures needed to rescue them.

It was too cold in the spacecraft for the astronauts to sleep except fitfully. On their last night in space, they donned two pairs of thermal underwear apiece to ward off the chill. Lovell even put on his bulky moonwalking shoes to keep his toes warm.

Picking up speed under the increasing pull of the earth's gravity, *Apollo* was now rapidly approaching its narrow reentry slot. Astronaut John Swigert took up his post in the command module pilot's seat. Looking out of the window he commented: "That earth is whistling in like a high-speed train."

At exactly 1:08 P.M., six days after its ill-starred journey began, *Apollo 13* splashed down in the South Pacific within view of the *Iwo Jima*'s decks about four miles away.

Forty-five minutes later, a helicopter ferried the three astronauts to the deck of the *Iwo Jima*, where they were greeted by cheers from sailors and a fitting tribute from the *Iwo Jima* band, Aquarius.

The safe return of the *Apollo 13* astronauts is witness to the fact that the prayers of people around the world were not in vain.

The editors of the *Wisconsin State Journal* did more than call upon God in a moment of desperation. They also remembered to express their appreciation following the splashdown of the *Apollo 13*. The next morning, Saturday, April 18, 1970, a giant banner in red letters shouted from the front page:

THANK GOD

Directly beneath this headline was a picture of the *Apollo 13* astronauts, Fred Haise, James Lovell, and John Swigert, as they stepped from the recovery helicopter to the carrier deck.

Another headline shouted, PRAYERS GO UP AS THREE COME DOWN.

The world welcomed the *Apollo 13* astronauts back to earth with tears, cheers, prayer, and praise. The President of the United States proclaimed Sunday, April 19, a national day of prayer and thanksgiving.

The American networks estimated that well over 125 million Americans watched sets in their homes and offices. Many witnessed the historic events in television showrooms or on giant screens such as the one in New York's Grand Central Terminal.

Prayers in hundreds of tongues followed the last hours of the space voyage. At the Virgin Mary Shrine of Divine Love outside Rome, relays of priests and laymen prayed in shifts. Pope Paul VI urged all to join him in prayer.

In his text proclaiming the National Day of Prayer and Thanksgiving, the President said, "The imperiled flight and safe return of the crew of *Apollo 13* were events that humbled and inspired people all over the world.

"We were inspired by the courage of the crew, the devotion and skill of the members of the NASA team on the ground, and by the offers of assistance from nations around the world.

"Particularly inspiring was the spontaneous outpouring of prayer, from every corner of the world, from members of every faith, calling upon God in His infinite mercy to bring home in safety to our small planet three fellow human beings.

"Now James A. Lovell, Jr., Fred. W. Haise, Jr., and John L. Swigert, Jr., are home again. The prayers of millions all over the world helped to bring them home safely.

"I urge my fellow Americans and all the peoples of the world to join with me in offering another prayer, one of deep thanks, for the safe return of the crew of the *Apollo 13.*"

When the *Apollo 13* astronauts returned to our planet, the very first item on their agenda as soon as they set foot on the deck of the recovery ship in the Pacific was a public prayer of thanksgiving. The cover picture of *Time* magazine for April 27, 1970, shows the three astronauts standing with heads bowed in prayer aboard the U.S.S. *Iwo Jima*.

Concerning *Apollo*'s return to earth, *Time* magazine said: "Perhaps the largest audience in history watched the return, participating through TV's intimacy in every moment of the final, fiery descent."

On June 21, 1970, astronaut John Swigert came to

Omaha for the "Spirit Of Apollo Days" and to take part in ground-breaking ceremonies for a new park on the west side of the city. It was my good luck to be in Omaha for the summer, teaching physics to Creighton University students. On the Sunday afternoon of the ground-breaking of the new park, to be called Tranquility Park, some of my students drove me out to see John Swigert.

Before astronaut John Swigert left his space-booted footprints in freshly poured cement in the center of Tranquility Park, he mounted a platform in the open field and gave one of the most direct and heartwarming talks I have ever heard. John Swigert emphasized how the experience of the *Apollo 13* astronauts made them realize more keenly than ever their dependence upon God. Swigert concluded his talk by saying, "I want to thank each of you for all the prayers you said that brought us back from the moon."

Astronaut James Lovell we met previously. He was one of the *Apollo 8* astronauts who orbited the moon at Christmastime in 1968. He is said to have had his eyes on the stars ever since he was a teenager in Milwaukee. When he entered Annapolis in 1948, he was allowed only one elective course, a language. Lovell chose German, and then used his newly acquired linguistic skill to read the writings of a then-little-known scientist by the name of Wernher von Braun.

Intrigued by von Braun's writings, Lovell himself was soon predicting some of the space-age flights that have since taken place. Unfortunately, Lovell's classmates did not share his vision. They replied to his dream with the taunt, "Lovell, some day you're going to the moon."

When Lovell first set foot back on planet Earth after the *Apollo 13* experience, he said, "We do not realize what we have on earth until we leave it."

The President of the United States summarized the reaction of many when he said, "The three astronauts did not reach the moon, but they reached the hearts of millions of people in America and in the world."

GIANT STEPS LEAVE PERMANENT IMPRINT

GIANT STEPS LEAVE PERMANENT IMPRINT
ON MOONWALKERS

ASTRONAUTS FIND FAITH ON SPACE TRIPS

GOD STILL IN CONTROL, SAYS ASTRONAUT

These were some of the headlines used by newspapers in summing up the results of the exciting years that brought Americans to the surface of the moon.

"I felt the power of God as I'd never felt it before," said astronaut James B. Irwin.

"It was an overwhelming experience," said Neil A. Armstrong, the first man on the moon.

A Baptist minister, Roger Lovette, said of the moonwalkers: "It has been interesting to read of the changes that have taken place in the lives of our astronauts when they change their point of view. Out in space, thousands of miles from this tiny planet, things become forever different. Suddenly diapers and braces and car payments and better homes and gardens do not count quite so much. The astronauts have come back to earth to become preachers and poets, novelists and evangelists."

Martin Caidin, a writer acquainted with many astronauts, told *American Baptist* magazine: "There has been a tremendous change, very quietly, in the attitudes and lives of men who have gone to the moon, where they can see the planet the way God must have seen it."

The reason for this change, according to Dr. Wernher von Braun, is that, in space, "evidences of a creator are so overwhelming." Astronaut James Irwin viewed his moon journey as such an overpowering religious experience that he felt compelled to tell others about it. He retired from the air force and NASA in 1972 and founded High Flight, an interdenominational evangelistic foundation headquartered in Colorado Springs, Colorado. On the speaking circuit, attesting to his faith, Irwin said that his moon visit constituted a "spiritual awakening" for him.

During the fall of 1973, astronaut James B. Irwin appeared in five midwestern states. The theme of his meetings was "The Now God." Irwin began his meetings on October 15 in Waupun, Wisconsin, and concluded them in Kalamazoo, Michigan, on October 25.

Irwin served as lunar module pilot for *Apollo 15*, which was the fourth moon-landing mission and the first to visit and explore the southeast edge of the Sea of Rains. Irwin described his twelve-day journey into space and his three-day stay on the moon's surface. He gave his personal testimony of how he met God on the moon and how this experience changed his life.

To me, one of the most exciting things of the Bicentennial Year was the talk that astronaut Irwin gave in Watertown, South Dakota. The man who left his footprints and offered his prayers on the moon, and the first American to explore the fabled Mountains of the Moon, told his eager audience, "No matter how far man removes himself from the earth, God is still in control."

Irwin said that the greatest consolation the astronauts had as the *Saturn 5* rocket boosted them into space "was knowing that we had the prayers of men and women everywhere. God became closer and closer to us as we ventured deeper and deeper into space," said Irwin. "I felt God's presence amid the grandeur of the moon."

Irwin showed the audience a fragment of the rare white moon rocks which he and his colleagues brought back despite the great odds against finding them. Irwin said that it was his conviction God was instrumental in leading the astronauts to them.

"We have seen and achieved great things in our country," said Irwin. "We have some problems, too, but I truly believe God can solve those problems if we'll but give our country back to Him."

Irwin went on to say that family relationships are the cornerstone of America's greatness and he asked his audience at the conclusion of his talk to reaffirm their faith in God and country.

Irwin admitted that when he blasted off for the moon atop the *Saturn 5* rocket he thought he was "just going up to get rocks and take some pictures." But, he said, he underwent many changes — psychological, spiritual, and physical.

The astronaut-turned-lay evangelist says, "I don't think man will return to the moon in our lifetime." On a somewhat different topic, he remarked: "I don't think extraterrestrial life has reached the earth yet. I don't think there is life [elsewhere] in our solar system . . . but I think there is life beyond."

Irwin freely admitted that the celebrity status he has achieved as one of the elite group of humans who have walked on the moon has had many benefits, but the demands put "a lot of stress on the husband-wife relationship." Even his children, he added, have both good and bad to say about their father's fame. Among the disadvantages is the fact that their peers, and sometimes even their teachers, put undue pressure on them.

In the summer of 1971 a study was made of the families of two men who had walked on the moon. The conclusion was that the rocket set differs markedly from the jet set. Old-time virtues shape the lives of the astronaut families of Colonel David R. Scott and Lieutenant Colonel James B. Irwin. They seem to possess elements of character that were first shaped in frontier America.

In both families the man is usually boss in the home. The children are strongly disciplined. The adults are generally — though not in every case — abstemious, rarely drinking, and still more rarely smoking. Some of them give little or no quarter to television.

They are buoyed up by strong religious beliefs, and they profess to lean as much on prayer as on technology when one of their members goes off to the moon.

Irwin and his wife choose not to have a television set in their home for themselves and their four children. Mary Irwin says she sees no sense in sitting her four children in front of television to watch people murder each other. There is too much violence on TV, she feels. An exception to a TV in their home was made during the flight of *Apollo 15*. As soon as the flight was over, Mrs. Irwin said of the TV set, "I can hardly wait to get it out of here."

On the first Saturday of the spaceflight, at the hour her husband was taking his first moonwalk, Mary Ellen Irwin stepped from her home to go to teach her weekly class of teenagers in the Sabbath school at the Pasadena Seventh-day Adventist Church. A bystander asked Mary Ellen, in evident surprise, whether she was not going to watch her husband's exploit. "Jim is doing his duty, and I must do mine," she said crisply, and moved on.

To Mrs. Irwin, the *Apollo 15* flight was, in a phrase, "God's mission."

Both Mrs. Irwin and Mrs. Scott express a sort of hazy contempt for the principles of women's liberation — hazy because their view of it is from a great distance. "I honestly haven't been able to figure out what they want to be liberated from," said Mrs. Irwin.

Irwin carried with him to the moon a copy of a scroll

signed by more than six hundred members of the Nassau Bay Baptist Church, pledging their prayers for a safe voyage.

The Scotts are members of St. Christopher's Episcopal Church, where the astronaut is a vestryman. "Religion to me is something very private," said Mrs. Scott, "but I would have to say my religious faith has given me strength."

It is interesting to note that there are generals on both sides of the Scott family. Mrs. Scott's father is Brigadier General Isaac W. Ott, USAF (retired), a former test pilot. The colonel's father is Brigadier General Tom W. Scott, also USAF (retired).

The astronaut's mother said that her two sons had received "paddling when they needed it." Brig. General Scott went on to say: "Both boys knew and understood that when we told them to do something or not to do something, we meant it. They were taught respect for their elders."

I found it fascinating to listen on TV to astronaut Scott calmly and confidently addressing mankind from the surface of the moon; yet, according to his father, the astronaut still says "Yes, sir" and "No, sir" to his elders.

Mrs. Irwin's mother, Mrs. Leland F. Monroe said, "We gave the children a lot of loving, but I never spared the rod. My folks brought me up carefully and strictly in a religious way, and I did the same with them. We didn't *send* them to church — we *took* them to church."

The wife of astronaut James Irwin says that she carries on a family tradition by using direct discipline. Her method, she said, is "the fanny, in contact with the hand. It works very well."

If anyone thinks that the children of the astronauts are being brought up on old-fashioned methods, it might be good to recall that one of the most popular books in America today is the one by Dr. James C. Dobson, associate clinical professor of pediatrics at the University of

Apollo 15 *crew members stand beneath mission emblem. Left to right: David R. Scott, commander; Alfred M. Worden, command module pilot; and James R. Irwin, lunar module pilot.* (NASA *photo)*

Southern California School of Medicine. The title is *Dare to Discipline*.

On October 29, 1976, the United Press came out with the gruesome statistic that more Americans were murdered during the first four years of this decade than were killed during the entire Vietnam War. Murder now ranks as a major cause of death in the United States. The killers are "typical Americans" with an average age of twenty-one. One out of every four murders is committed by a woman. Seventy percent of the victims are friends or relatives of their killers!

Dr. Donald T. Lunde, clinical associate professor of psychiatry and law at Stanford University, says that our nation is in the middle of a murder epidemic unparalleled in history. The reason for the rising tide of murder in this country, according to Dr. Lunde, is that today's generation of children is encouraged to act out hostilities and externalize restraints to a degree that someone else is always responsible for their failures.

"These young," said Dr. Lunde, "were raised differently from past generations. There has been more affluence, more permissiveness."

THE HAWSER
OF FAITH, USA

By making open profession of their faith and the power of prayer, the astronauts and men of the space age have brought religion to the attention of the world. In so doing, they have, so to speak, brought God into focus in the minds of millions.

By their references to God, the astronauts remind us of the hawser of faith that runs through our history. They remind us that our country is based on God. They remind us of the faith that made America.

In no other nation's founding documents can we find so many declarations of allegiance to God, dependence upon His guidance, and appeals to the "Supreme Judge" in seeking to build a new nation. According to the Reverend Billy Graham, no other nation on earth is so firmly rooted in its religious heritage. This spiritual resource remains our greatest strength.

When our Founding Fathers in 1776 drew up and adopted a charter, now recognized as one of the noblest documents of all time, they based its authority on Almighty God.

In so brief a document these men might have made but one reference to Almighty God, but they wanted to hammer home truths which they feared others might discard, truths which they knew were fundamental to democracy. Woven, therefore, into the texture of the Declaration of Independence are four significant sentences, two at the beginning, and two at the end.

In the first section they establish their claims for a new nation on the laws of God. And they emphasize the fact that the natural law itself depends on God.

They then go on to say that they hold these truths to be self-evident: "That all men are created equal, that they are endowed by their Creator with certain unalienable Rights."

Towards the end of the document the Founding Fathers appeal to "the Supreme Judge of the world" for the rectitude of their intentions.

The Declaration closes with the following statement: "And for the support of this Declaration, with a firm reliance on the protection of divine Providence, we mutually pledge to each other, our Lives, our Fortunes, and our sacred Honor."

Evidently the Fathers of our country felt they should be most explicit. They were men who believed firmly in God. They were men aware that the idea of God had to be integrated with everything if we were not to forget that our rights, our liberties, our very lives come from the Creator.

Congress was as anxious as the men who framed the Declaration. They didn't want Americans in the generations ahead to forget for one moment that human rights come from the Source of all rights and not out of the thin atmosphere.

This doctrine was nothing new to the Founding Fathers and to Congress. They knew it had come down through long, history-packed centuries; that for thousands of years, despite persecution and obstacles of every sort, the Jews had kept alive the sublime concept that man comes from God, that he derives his rights from his Creator, and that, because of this, he has a solemn obligation to each of his fellowmen, in whom he should see a child of God.

For the Founding Fathers, the firm basis of individual and social conduct was faith in God and a conscience responsive to His Commandments. The truth is that America was built on principles of human dignity derived from the Judeo-Christian view of man.

"A world in Flames, and a whole System tumbling in Ruins to the Center, has nothing terrifying in it to a man whose Security is builded on the adamantine Basis of good Conscience and confirmed Piety." So wrote John Adams in his diary in 1756 at the age of twenty.

In his *Notes on the State of Virginia*, Thomas Jefferson wrote in 1785, at the age of forty-two: "And can the liberties of a nation be thought secure when we have removed their only firm basis, a conviction in the minds of the people that these liberties are the gift of God? That they are not to be violated but with his wrath?"

Thomas Jefferson was a rare genius whose inventions may be seen at Monticello, the hilltop home he designed and built in Virginia. It is truly a work of art, and a joy to behold. I spent a fascinating afternoon there some years ago.

The sage of Monticello described himself as a believer in God who drew from his faith the conviction that God had given freedom to the human person.

The faith of Jefferson is also evidenced by his compilation of *The Jefferson Bible*, in which he assembled into one chronological account the story of Jesus as told in the four Gospels.

When astronauts on their way to the moon atop a *Saturn 5* rocket uttered a quick prayer for God's help, they were — in a certain sense — carrying on a wonderful tradition of "instant prayer" inaugurated by our first president.

When George Washington took the oath as first president of the United States on April 30, 1789, he spontaneously added this prayer of his own: "So help me God."

It is interesting to note that this invocation is still used in official oaths by those taking public office, in courts of justice, and in other legal proceedings.

In the first part of his *Inaugural Address*, immediately following the oath, Washington reverently acknowledged our country's dependence on Almighty God.

"It would be peculiarly improper to omit in this first official act," Washington said, "my fervent supplications to that Almighty Being who rules over the universe — who presides in the council of nations — and whose providential aids can supply every human defect, that His benediction may consecrate to the liberties and happiness of the people of the United States a government instituted by themselves for these essential purposes."

Seven and half years later, on September 19, 1796, Washington gave his memorable *Farewell Address*. In it, he gave public testimony to the importance of religion and morality in the conduct of good government.

"Of all the dispositions and habits which lead to political prosperity," our first president said, "religion and morality are indispensable supports."

Then, in his next sentence, he questioned the patriotism of those who would banish religious truth from public affairs: "In vain would that man claim the tribute of patriotism, who should labor to subvert these great pillars of human happiness, these firmest props of the destinies of men and citizens." Continuing in the same vein, Washington maintained that we would endanger the very security and survival of our nation if we forgot, ignored, or failed to teach the intimate connection between religion and morality: "Let it simply be asked, where is the security for property, for reputation, for life, if the sense of religious obligations desert the oaths which are the instruments of investigation in courts of justice?

"And let us with caution indulge the supposition that morality can be maintained without religion.

"Whatever may be conceded to the influence of refined education on minds of peculiar structure, reason and experience both forbid us to expect that national morality can prevail in exclusion of religious principle."

Few Americans realize how clearly and repeatedly George Washington insisted that our freedom as a nation has its origin in God and will endure only so long as this basic truth is recognized and cherished.

Note that Washington's concept of separation of Church and State was a healthy, balanced one. While no Church was to dominate the State, our dependence on God must be duly recognized, not only privately, but in government and school life as well. It was furthest from his mind that the agnosticism or atheism of a small minority be imposed on the great majority.

On June 20, 1775, Washington was commissioned by the first Continental Congress to be commander-in-chief of the Colonial army. "The time is now near at hand," Washington gravely reminded his troops, "which must probably determine whether Americans are to be freemen or slaves; whether they are to have any property they can call their own. The fate of unborn millions will now depend, under God, on the courage and conduct of this army.

"Let us therefore rely on the goodness of the cause and the aid of the Supreme Being, in whose hands victory is, to animate and encourage us to great and noble actions."

On July 9, 1776, Washington said, "The blessing and protection of Heaven are at all times necessary, but especially so in times of public danger."

For the next eighteen months, reverses, misfortunes, and trials plagued the commander-in-chief. These culminated in the almost unbearable winter at Valley Forge and in the defeat at the Battle of Monmouth. Yet his faith and perseverance remained unshaken. In a letter to General Nelson, written on August 20, 1778, he said: "Providence has been so conspicuous in all this, that he must be worse than an infidel that lacks faith, and more than wicked that has not gratitude enough to acknowledge his obligations."

Washington's hope amid defeat was paralleled by his gratitude and humility in success. After the decisive victory at Yorktown, Virginia, October 19, 1781, he wrote a friend in Connecticut: "To the great Ruler of Events and not to any service of mine, I ascribe the termination of our contest for liberty. I never considered the fortunate issue of any measure adopted by me in the progress of the Revolution in any other light than as the ordering of Divine Providence."

The peace treaty with England was signed on September 3, 1783. A few months later, Washington resigned the commission he had held for eight years. At noon on December 23, he appeared before Congress, and, thinking his years of public service had at last come to an end, he addressed the assembled members. "I consider it an indispensable duty," he said, "to close this last solemn act of my official life by commending the interests of our dearest Country to the protection of Almighty God, and those who have the superintendence of them to His holy keeping."

The conditions Washington found when he returned to Mount Vernon were far from ideal. The farm was no longer on a paying basis, and he owed money for taxes. But despite such problems, he was glad to be home. In 1784 he sent a message to General Knox. "I feel now . . . as I conceive a weary traveller must do," he wrote, "who, after treading many a painful step, with a heavy burden on his shoulders, is eased of the latter, having reached the goal to which all the former were directed, and from his housetop is looking back, and tracing with a grateful eye the meanders by which he escaped the quicksands and mires which lay in his way; and into which none but the All-powerful Guide and Great Disposer of human events could have prevented his falling."

A month after his inauguration, Washington avowed his impartial support of "vital religion." Addressing the bishops of the Methodist Episcopal Church in New York

117

City on May 29, 1789, he said : "I trust the people of every denomination who demean themselves as good citizens will have occasion to be convinced that I shall always strive to prove a faithful and impartial Patron of genuine, vital religion."

As the first president, Washington was aware that his actions could well become precedents. On October 3, 1789, he proclaimed a national Thanksgiving Day. This was the beginning of a long series of similar executive orders that have remained part of American life down to the present. "Whereas it is the duty," Washington said, "of all nations to acknowledge the Providence of Almighty God, to obey His will, to be grateful for His benefits, and humbly to implore His protection and favor, and whereas both Houses of Congress have by their joint committee requested me to commend to the people of the United States a day of public thanksgiving and prayer to be observed by acknowledging with grateful hearts the many signal favors of Almighty God, especially by affording them an opportunity peaceably to establish a form of government for their safety and happiness, now therefore I do recommend and assign Thursday the 26th day of November next, to be devoted to the service of that great and glorious Being, Who is the beneficent Author of all the good that was, that is, or will be."

An influential and talented man in early America was Benjamin Franklin. His intellectual curiosity led him to conduct electrical experiments by flying a kite into a thunderstorm. He also invented bifocal eyeglasses not unlike those we wear today, the Franklin stove, and many other devices.

Franklin's spiritual influence was of historic proportions. It was his exhortation to prayer that broke deadlock over Congressional representation at the Constitutional Convention in Philadelphia in 1787, when he rose and addressed the group.

"Gentlemen," he said, "I have lived a long time and

am convinced that God governs the affairs of men. If a sparrow cannot fall to the ground without His notice, is it probable that an empire can rise without His aid?

"I, therefore, move that prayers imploring the assistance of Heaven be held every morning before we proceed to business."

It was not long before a compromise was reached and the United States Constitution was born — borne on the wings of prayer.

Franklin outlined his personal religious creed to Ezra Stiles in a letter written just before his death. "Here is my creed," he wrote. "I believe in one God, Creator of the Universe. That He governs it by His providence. That He ought to be worshipped. That the most acceptable service we render Him is doing good to His other children."

Our second president, John Adams, believed in the existence of a personal God based on such evidence as "the amazing harmony of our solar system" and "the stupendous plan of operation."

It is fascinating to note that his words could well be those of our astronauts, John Glenn or Frank Borman. John Adams followed the exhortation of Psalm 145: "Every day will I bless you, and I will praise your name forever and ever. Great is the Lord and highly to be praised; his greatness is unsearchable. Generation after generation praises your works and proclaims your might. They speak of the splendor of your glorious majesty and tell of your wondrous works."

Not many years before his death, Adams wrote to an old friend: "I am not tormented with the fear of death. A kind Providence has preserved and supported me for eighty-five years and seven months, through many dangers and difficulties. I am not afraid to trust its goodness to all eternity."

Adams died at ninety on the same day Thomas Jefferson died, the fiftieth anniversary of the Declaration of Independence.

Our fourth president, James Madison, excelled in biblical courses as a graduate student at Princeton, especially in Hebrew language studies. He continued his theological studies throughout his life. In the field of religion, James Madison was first and foremost an advocate of freedom of worship. Madison held "that religion, or the duty which we owe to our Creator and the manner of discharging it, can be directed only by reason and conviction, not by force or violence; and therefore, that all men should enjoy the fullest toleration in the exercise of religion, according to the dictates of conscience."

The strength of American life is rooted deep as an oak tree in Christian truth. An editorial in *Fortune* magazine testifies: "The basic teachings of Christianity are in its bloodstream. The central doctrine of its political system — the sacredness of the individual — is a doctrine inherited from nineteen hundred years of Christian insistence on the immortality of the soul."

From the beginnings of our national existence, our forefathers sought to form a society almost unique in human history, a society of free men under God for the protection of the equal rights of all. The basic bond of union was the willing recognition of mutual rights and reciprocal duties.

Each of the Old World peoples who had part in the building of our New World commonwealth brought here a strong religious piety which powerfully influenced our national character and our civil traditions.

Even our money bears witness to the fact that ours is a God-founded nation, and it emphasizes the additional fact that as a nation we rely upon Divine Providence.

On the dollar bill is a pyramid, which represents the building of our country. The fact that it is broken emphasizes that our nation is not yet completed. If you look on the left-hand side of a greenback, you will find, directly above the pyramid, an eye. This symbolizes the all-seeing God and stresses the importance of putting spiritual welfare above material prosperity. Our Founding Fathers believed that our strength was rooted in God and that our progress must always be under the watchful eye of Providence.

Directly above the eye on the green side of the dollar bill you will find the words *Annuit Coeptis* in a semicircle at the top of the seal. The words *Annuit Coeptis* signify: "He (God) has smiled on our undertakings."

The three Latin words that appear directly under the pyramid mean, "A new order of the ages." This statement suggests that our nation, under God, is introducing a new age in the life and freedom of mankind. The American seal was approved by Congress on June 20, 1782.

Abraham Lincoln included in many of his public addresses references to Almighty God. Notable among them is the closing passage of his *Farewell Address* at Springfield, Illinois, on February 11, 1861, as he prepared to take up the presidency. "Without the assistance of that Divine Being," said Lincoln, "I cannot succeed. With that assistance I cannot fail. Trusting in Him who can go with me and remain with you and be everywhere for good, let us confidently hope that all will yet be well."

Every time you sing "The Star-spangled Banner" you recall the fact that our nation "hath been made and preserved" by God. It was during the bombardment of Fort McHenry on the night of September 13, 1814, that Francis Scott Key composed "The Star-spangled Banner." For 117 years, this song was popular as a patriotic hymn. On March 3, 1931, Congress adopted "The Star-spangled Banner" as our national anthem. It closes with these words: "Praise the Power that hath made and preserved us a nation. Then conquer we must, when our cause it is just. And this be our motto — 'In God is our trust.' "

On July 20, 1956, a joint resolution was adopted by Congress establishing "In God We Trust" as the national motto of the United States.

Our pledge to the flag is an affirmation incorporating

the basic principles of America, namely, that we are one nation indivisible, formed and existing under Divine Providence.

On April 20, 1953, a resolution was introduced in the House of Representatives to add the words "under God" to the pledge of allegiance to the flag.

Both the House of Representatives and the Senate adopted the resolution. It became law when President Eisenhower signed the bill on June 14, 1954.

The pledge of allegiance now reads: "I pledge allegiance to the flag of the United States of America and to the Republic for which it stands; one nation under God, indivisible, with liberty and justice for all."

In the frightful days of World War II when cannon were booming across the world, Franklin D. Roosevelt, a vestryman of his church, enumerated the Four Freedoms, which are firmly based on the religious convictions that were his: "In the future days, which we seek to make secure, we look forward to a world founded upon four essential human freedoms. The first is freedom of speech and expression — everywhere in the world. The second is freedom of every person to worship God in his own way — everywhere in the world. The third is freedom from want. . . . The fourth is freedom from fear."

Before his inauguration in 1953, Dwight D. Eisenhower made a pilgrimage with his family and Cabinet members and their wives to a church service.

Soon after the inauguration, Eisenhower introduced the first Presidential Prayer Breakfast, an event that has been sponsored every year by all presidents since.

In his stirring *Challenge*, delivered at a meeting of the Freedom Foundation, President Eisenhower emphasized the fact that our country emerged from religious origins.

"If we are to win the hearts and beliefs of men," Eisenhower said, "we have to go back to fundamentals. Our Founding Fathers said it was a religious concept they were trying to translate into the political world.

"Our form of government has no sense unless it is founded in a deeply felt religious faith. If we can be strong enough to sell this idea, no false theory, such as Communism, can make any headway. We will be more confident of peace and more certain that we can pass on to our grandchildren the kind of life which does not guarantee them riches, but which does guarantee them opportunity to live in dignified fashion with their God and their fellow citizens."

It is interesting to note that the Supreme Court recognizes that belief in God is an integral part of American life. In one section of its majority opinion the Court testifies: "The fact that the Founding Fathers believed devotedly that there was a God and that the unalienable rights of man were rooted in Him is clearly evidenced in their writings, from the Mayflower Compact to the Constitution itself. This background is evidenced today in our public life through the continuance in our oaths of office, from the presidency to the alderman, of the final supplication, 'so help me God.'

"Likewise each house of the Congress provides through its chaplain an opening prayer, and the sessions of this Court are declared open by the crier in a short ceremony, the final phrase of which invokes the grace of God.

"It can be truly said, therefore, that today, as in the beginning, our national life reflects a religious people who, in the words of Madison, are 'earnestly praying, as . . . in duty bound, that the Supreme Lawgiver of the universe . . . guide them into every measure which may be worthy of His . . . blessing.' "

When Gerald Ford was president, he reminded us that "the Constitution is the supreme law of our land and it governs our actions as citizens. Only the laws of God, which govern our consciences, are superior to it.

"As we are a nation under God, so I am sworn to uphold our laws with the help of God."

It is interesting to note that when Columbus set sail for the New World, he did so proudly proclaiming his belief in God and asking for divine help.

The astronauts, cruising out into the new world of space, likewise proclaimed their belief in God and asked for God's help.

From Columbus sailing the ocean blue in 1492 to astronauts sailing through the vastness of space in our twentieth century, religious convictions have been woven into the fabric of life in America.

May the exploits of the men of our space age help bring into focus the heritage of faith that is ours here in America.

Perhaps we might make our own the prayer which Thomas Jefferson recited each day of his eight years as president, and every day thereafter until his death: "Almighty God, Who has given us this good land for our heritage, we humbly beseech Thee that we may always prove ourselves a people mindful of Thy favor and glad to do Thy will. Bless our land with honorable industry, sound learning, and pure manners.

"Endow with the spirit of wisdom those to whom in Thy name we entrust the authority of government, that there may be justice and peace at home, and that, through obedience to Thy law, we may show forth Thy praise among the nations of the earth.

"In time of prosperity, fill our hearts with thankfulness, and, in the day of trouble, suffer not our Trust in Thee to fail; all of which we ask through Jesus Christ, our Lord, Amen."

If ever you are in Washington, D.C., and want to see a concrete reminder of how the history of our country is interwoven with the lives of men of faith and prayer, visit the Washington Cathedral.

The cathedral is the dream of George Washington come alive in soaring arches of stone that leap skyward as though they never heard of the law of gravity.

Born in the mind of George Washington in the 1790s, revived by Protestant laymen a century later, chartered by Congress in 1893, begun in 1907, Washington's Cathedral of Saint Peter and Saint Paul is still a decade or more from completion.

The twin towers will rise 230 feet. The central *Gloria in Excelsis* tower was finished in 1964. The top of the central tower is the highest point in Washington, 676 feet above sea level, eighty feet higher than the Washington Monument.

Each bay and cornice inside the cathedral seems to highlight a point of American history. A statue of George Washington recalls the first president who expressed the hope that the highest hill in the new capital city would become the site for "a church for all Americans."

Although the cathedral is the seat of the Episcopal bishop of Washington, it has been interdenominational. Virtually every major faith has held services in the cathedral.

It was entirely fitting that the funeral service for Dr. Wernher von Braun was held in the Washington Cathedral. The cathedral has a "space window" dedicated to the achievements of America's astronauts. A moon rock, brought back by the crew of *Apollo 11*, is incorporated in the window.

At the start of the service, Dean Francis B. Sayre intoned the words, "If I take the wings of the morning." It was, indeed, the vision and drive of Wernher von Braun that gave us the wings to carry our astronauts to the moon.

At the end of the service, it may have been one's imagination or simply the play of sunlight upon it, but the moon rock brought back by the *Apollo 11* astronauts and set in the stained-glass window in the cathedral's nave seemed to glow while the tolling of the great bells reminded the people of the passing of the spirit of von Braun into that infinity which had always challenged his soaring imagination.

125

A SPIN-OFF
OF WONDER

To me, one of the greatest spin-offs of the Apollo project has been an awakening of our sense of wonder — not only in the marvels of space, but in all things.

The photos brought back by our astronauts gave us new vistas of beauty and awoke our curiosity to the grandeur of God as manifest in all creation.

When the first men to orbit the moon addressed a synod of bishops in Rome, a cardinal asked the astronauts whether their unprecedented view of physical creation had had any effect on their spiritual lives. They replied in words reminiscent of these from the Book of Wisdom: "For from the greatness and the beauty of created things their original author, by analogy, is seen."

The example of the astronauts reminds us not only to regard the world of nature as beautiful in itself, but with that reverence that Cardinal Newman defined as "belief in God's presence."

The poet Gerard Manley Hopkins emphasized the incarnational awareness that relishes the beauty of things because it knows they emanate from God and refers them back to their Author. Hopkins cries out: "Give beauty back, beauty, beauty, beauty, back to God, beauty's self and beauty's giver."

For Hopkins, all life was a wonderful revelation. As he wrote in one of his sermons: "All things are charged with love, are charged with God, and, if we know how to touch them, give off sparks and take fire, yield drops and flow."

As in the beginning of creation, God's living Spirit still hovers, broods over the world — a world vibrating with beauty and singing its praise to God.

No wonder the Royal Psalmist sings: "It is good to give thanks to the Lord, to sing praise to your name, Most High, to proclaim your kindness at dawn and your faithfulness throughout the night. . . . For you make me glad, O Lord, by your deeds; at the works of your hands I rejoice."

"In joy shall you depart . . ." said the prophet Isaiah. "Mountains and hills shall break out in song before you, and all the trees of the countryside shall clap their hands."

Einstein informs us that the most wonderful thing we can experience in this world is the mysterious — that which leads us to wonder. This sense of wonder and the ability to thrill to the beauty of creation is the source of all true art, science, and religion. If we but come alive to the beauty and the marvels of the universe around us, we shall be led to God, who is the most radiant beauty and the highest wisdom.

Dag Hammarskjold reminds us that "We die on the day when our lives cease to be illumined by the steady radiance, renewed daily, of a wonder, the source of which is beyond all reason."

I was delighted with what I learned on a beautiful evening in the spring of 1978. Father Tom Smith, the pastor of Saint Patrick's Church in Seneca, Wisconsin, had invited me to take part in the Confirmation ceremonies. Following the Confirmation, Bishop F. W. Freking of La Crosse gave a beautiful, inspiring talk in which he mentioned that among the Gifts of the Holy Spirit, the gift formerly known as "fear of the Lord" is now called "the gift of wonder and awe."

127

How truly appropriate and magnificent. "Wonder," says Thomas Carlyle, "is the basis of worship."

E. B. Browning tells us, "Earth's crammed with heaven, and every common bush afire with God."

"To be surprised, to wonder," says José Ortega y Gasset, "is to begin to understand."

No doubt you have experienced moments in your life when the God of creation moved in close and momentarily touched you with His presence through some natural happening. It might have been something as simple and lovely as a tree standing tall and solitary, reaching up to the heavens from a windswept plain. It might have been an ocean shore with the waves crashing in with tireless power and majesty. It might have been a spring day with its sweet promise of fresh life after the exhaustion of winter.

Such experiences have value in bringing us fleetingly close to God. "Use your eyes," wrote Helen Keller, "as if tomorrow you would be stricken blind; hear the music of voices, the song of a bird, as if you would be stricken deaf tomorrow. Touch each object as if tomorrow your tactile sense would fail. Smell the perfume of flowers, taste with relish each morsel as if tomorrow you could never smell and taste again."

To enjoy the wonder that should be yours, seek the occasions and seize the day as a child does. Come ride the wind when it blows and follow, follow to where it goes. Your friends shall be the river and the trees, the sun that laughs and marches, the swallows and the sea.

In *Childe Harold's Pilgrimage*, Lord Byron tells us:

There is a pleasure in the pathless woods,
There is a rapture on the lonely shore,
There is a society, where none intrudes,
By the deep sea, and music in its roar:
I love not Man the less, but Nature more,
From these our interviews, in which I steal

From all I may be, or have been before,
To mingle with the universe, and feel
What I can ne'er express, yet cannot all conceal.

Roll on, thou deep and dark blue ocean — roll!
Thou glorious mirror, where the Almighty's form
Glasses itself in tempests; in all time,
Calm or convulsed — in breeze or gale, or storm,
Icing the pole, or in the torrid clime
Dark-heaving; boundless, endless, and sublime —
The image of eternity — the throne
Of the Invisible; even from out thy slime
The monsters of the deep are made: each zone
Obeys thee: thou goest forth, dread, fathomless, alone.

And I have loved thee, Ocean! and my joy
Of youthful sports was on thy breast to be
Borne, like thy bubbles, onward: from a boy
I wantoned with thy breakers — they to me
Were a delight; and if the freshening sea
Made them a terror — 'twas a pleasing fear,
For I was as it were a child of thee,
And trusted to thy billows far and near,
And laid my hand upon thy mane — as I do here.

Joan Mills tells us that she loves to walk along the ocean's shore when great waves leap toward the land, thunderously breaking, flinging wild arcs of spray upward. So great is the ecstasy of her wonder that Joan exclaims: "I cannot help what so often transpires in me when I experience the majesties of the world — that inward reeling and joyful humility, that inarticulate private praising. The only word that I can put to what I feel is *love*. And never do I feel that intemperate ardor more than when I yield my senses to the enormous presence of the sea."

When I visited Hawaii in August 1963, I found that the sea for untold ages had spoken to the people of God.

129

The Hawaiians have a respect and reverence for the sea. Born ecologists, they lived in harmony with nature. In Hawaii, this study of the sea and its waves is called *ka nalu*, a concept that includes seeing, feeling, and sensing the rhythms of the sea as well as the unity between man and the sea.

A man who looked upon the beauty of sea and sky as being a reflection of God was St. Bonaventure. St. Bonaventure was born in Tuscany in 1221, five years before the death of St. Francis of Assisi. As a teenager he went to Paris, became a friar, and studied under the famous English Franciscan, Alexander of Hales. His teaching career at the University of Paris was cut short when he was selected to be superior general of the fast-growing Franciscan order. Later he became a bishop, a cardinal, and a guiding light at the Council of Lyons, during which he died on July 15, 1274.

St. Bonaventure looked upon the material world as a stairway to God. The destiny of the created universe is to reveal the beauty of God, who expresses himself in it. And so, for Bonaventure, all the things of nature — butterflies, mountains, cherry trees — call out to us as if to say: "Take note of us, for we are messengers to speak to you of God's beauty."

According to Bonaventure, our sense of wonder will lead to gratitude and joy.

Bonaventure shows us a world coming forth from God as from an overflowing fountain, a harmonious world reflecting the beauty of God, a world that beckons to us to praise God in his creatures.

If we take to heart the advice of St. Bonaventure, we shall shout with joy the words of Psalm 139: "For all these mysteries I thank you, for the wonder of myself, for the wonder of your works."

The Russian novelist Fyodor Dostoyevski, in a prayer of extraordinary sensitivity, touches the mystery and wonder of God's presence in all of nature:

Lord, may I love all Thy creation,
The whole and every grain of sand in it.
May I love every leaf, every ray of light.
For I acknowledge unto Thee that all is like an ocean,
All is flowing and blending,
And that to withhold any measure of love
From anything in Thy universe
Is to withhold the same measure from Thee.

According to Father Joseph T. Nolan, "We cannot hold in — nor should we — the sudden shout of gladness or exultation at the discovery that we are loved and that life is good. The yell can turn into the *Gloria* of a Mozart, the great symphonic music of Beethoven, or the lyrics of Shelley praising a skylark."

It is in this joyful spirit that Maureen Cannon exults:

> *March meanders*
> *out-of-doors*
> *Till it stumbles on*
> *a . . . crocus.*
> *What a lovely*
> *hokus-pokus*
> *To have such a tiny thing*
> *As a purple crocus poke*
> > *us*
> > *Into Spring!*

Baron Friedrich von Hugel was greatly and delightedly a Catholic. He integrated all aspects of his life in the search for God's kingdom. To discover God in people made him rejoice like Saint Francis at the sheer exuberance of divine love.

Friedrich von Hugel was born in 1852 and died in 1925. His profound respect for people and his sensitivity to truth and goodness wherever he met them made him revere the presence of God in every faith.

To von Hugel, religion was a delight and a glory. He was

self-disciplined and even ascetic, but he had a huge capacity for enjoyment and a power to evoke it in others.

He insisted over and over again that a proper Christian life must include other than religious interests, and his own passionate interest in geology, butterflies, and many other things are examples of this. In them all, he found God, not because he looked for "edification," but simply because God was there in the sheer reality of "the particular tone of my brother's voice, the leaping of my dog in the grass, the scent of apricot on the old, red-brick, sun-baked wall, the iridescence of this opal, the sound of the grinding of the pebbles on yonder seashore."

"It seems to me," says Mel Ellis, "that God is best reflected in the sun coming through pure air to shine brightly on a clean, sparkling stream. It seems to me that the Creator's majesty can never be better exemplified than in the soaring heights of an uncluttered mountain."

Religion has been defined as a deep awareness of God as the basis of all things. It is a response to reality apprehended as divine. When God is seen everywhere, there is two-way communication, perhaps the highest form of worship.

A priest-friend of mine once remarked: "Religion seems to me primarily an aesthetic thing, not in the sense that it is a self-fulfilling experience or a search for pleasure, but in the sense that it is, ideally, an *almost unfree response to overwhelming beauty*. It is, as Baron von Hugel succinctly stated, 'pure adoration.'

"More and more," my friend concluded, "I find music the purest expression of religion and the greatest stimulus to devotion."

Edward J. Lavin informs us that "The saint sees God in all things. The light of God shines through every particle of the universe."

Centuries ago Saint Augustine said, "What beauty lies hidden in the wisdom of God! From it alone do all things derive beauty which appeals to our eyes."

According to John Muir, "Everybody needs beauty as well as bread, places to play in and pray in, where nature may heal and cheer and give strength to body and soul alike." Half Dome and the Merced River, Yosemite National Park. (TWA *photo*)

The ancient philosopher Plato knew that "in facing beauty, wings grow in our souls." One way God reveals Himself to us is through beauty. It is no exaggeration to say that by beauty man is borne up to God.

A long time ago in far distant Persia, a gentleman by the name of Abu al-Ghazali wisely observed: "The perception of beauty is a delight in itself which is loved for its own sake. And if it is certain that God is Beauty, he must be loved by that one to whom his beauty and majesty are revealed."

Closer to our own day, that famed man of the mountains, John Muir, informed us, "Everybody needs beauty as well as bread, places to play in and pray in where nature may heal and cheer and give strength to body and soul alike."

Father Kevin Coughlin reminds us that man needs to see beauty. The more beauty a man sees, the more beautiful he becomes. The beauty of the world and the beauty of man reflect the beauty of God. The more man sees the beauty around him, the closer he will be to seeing the beauty of God.

Fortunately for us, "Nature is painting for us, day after day, pictures of infinite beauty if only we have the eyes to see them." So says John Ruskin.

To experience and reflect on the goodness of reality is a compliment to God. The more man accepts himself as he is, the easier it is for him to accept God. The more man affirms the goodness of life, the more hope he will have in himself and in his future.

Bliss Carmen took a day off to search for God, and found Him "Just where one scarlet lily flamed, I saw his footprint in the sod."

The poet-priest, Father John Banister Tabb, wrote:

I see Thee in the distant blue;
But in the violet's dell of dew,
Behold, I breathe and touch Thee too.

134

Joseph Mary Plunkett, one of the Irish martyrs of the Easter Revolution of 1916, tells us:

I see his blood upon the rose
And in the stars the glory of his eyes,
His body gleams amid eternal snows,
His tears fall from the skies.
I see his face in every flower;
The thunder and the singing of the birds
Are but his voice – and carven by his power,
Rocks are his written words.
All pathways by his feet are worn,
His strong heart stirs the ever-beating sea.

"When it comes down to it," says Sidney Callahan, "I guess I'm seeking and finding God 'in all the old familiar places,' as the familiar song says. To me the beautiful world, flawed as it may be, is the first sign of God's presence."

"Always around us," says E. Merrill Root, "lies a world that can become either dull with habit and sleep, or magical with marvel and wonder."

Love comes to the heart that loves; beauty comes to the seekers of beauty. As you feel wonder, marvelous things happen around you and within you. According to G.K. Chesterton, "The world will never perish for lack of wonders, but only for lack of wonder." The fortunate people are those who never lose their sense of wonder.

Dr. Wernher von Braun was a man of wonder. He was a genius who saw visions and hammered them out upon the anvil of his mind into a reality that leaped out beyond the bounds of planet Earth. "Man belongs," he once said, "wherever he wants to go." And where von Braun wanted to go was out among the stars, to an orderly kingdom of relentlessly cold beauty based on the exact laws of physics.

Von Braun admitted that wonder and curiosity were the mainsprings behind his scientific research. He loved to quote Ralph Waldo Emerson, who said, "Men love to wonder, and that is the seed of science."

On May 12, 1977, I was most fortunate in obtaining a wonderful insight into the character of Dr. Wernher von Braun. I had been invited to come to the Pick Congress Hotel in Chicago to give the keynote address at the twenty-fourth International Technical Communication Conference. The title of my talk was "The Wonder of Words: An Adventure in Technical Communication."

At the banquet which followed my keynote address, I found myself at table with several people who had worked with Dr. Wernher von Braun. From them I learned that von Braun's sense of wonder kept him forever looking for the surprise that lies in everything and everybody. Everything in the world he found exciting. Everyone he met stimulated and roused his interest. He flung his powerful frame about with the abandon of an excited youngster at his first picnic or circus.

Von Braun's personal enthusiasms were what made life for him so zestful. It kept him eternally young. It kept him alive, alert, a man of unlimited interests, of constantly widening vistas, of friends beyond counting and knowledge wide, varied, and deep.

Von Braun found the whole world a place of magic and mystery and surprise and delights, of glorious revelations of man's wonderful nature, of astounding glimpses of the glory of the world's Creator. His enthusiasm for this world brought him to the feet of the world's Creator.

According to close associates who saw von Braun shortly before his death, he retained his mental faculties until the very end, recalling past travels and achievements.

Ever the intellectual seeker, von Braun had once remarked that he hoped he would retain at death sufficient clarity of mind so that he could enjoy to the full his flight from planet Earth into God's heavenly kingdom.

The year following the death of Dr. Wernher von Braun I had a most unusual opportunity to obtain a still deeper insight into the personality of this magnificent man.

At 4:00 P.M. on Friday afternoon, July 28, 1978, I was coming out of the post office in Prairie du Chien, Wisconsin. As I was walking down the steps, I noticed a car pull over to the curb. A man I knew in the parish leaned out the driver's window and shouted. "Father Scott! You are always talking about the astronauts in your sermons. Now you have a chance to meet one. I would like you to shake hands with my nephew, astronaut James A. McDivitt."

The blood vessels in my temples were ticking like metronomes, and my heart beating like bongo drums when I stretched out my hand to greet the handsome astronaut whose fame has gone down in space history.

James A. McDivitt proved to be a most fascinating and delightful person. He made me feel right at home. He patiently answered my many questions — questions which, I'm sure, he must have been asked countless times by other people. All too swiftly the time flew by and I had to say goodbye to my wonderful, newfound friend.

When he returned to his president's office at the Pullman Standard in Chicago, James McDivitt sent me a charming letter in which he said, "It was a real pleasure to have the opportunity to meet you in Prairie du Chien. It was such a coincidence because, as my Uncle Raymond mentioned, we were talking about you only thirty minutes before that time, and just a minute or so before seeing you he commented that it would be nice to speak to you. As if directed by the Good Lord, our paths crossed."

In my exciting conversation with McDivitt, I asked him whether or not he had ever met Dr. Wernher von Braun. Jim informed me that he had the honor many times. The first time was long before there was even a space program. In this talk von Braun shared with others his dream of going to the moon.

At this time, James McDivitt informed me that he, himself, was a test pilot, and he had not the faintest idea that one day he would be an astronaut heading out into space.

McDivitt said that Dr. Wernher von Braun was a gifted genius whose brilliant intellect fashioned the *Saturn 5* rocket that brought our astronauts to the moon.

Then James McDivitt went on to say something most important: "I know that Dr. Wernher von Braun is given credit for his intellectual ability and his skill as an outstanding scientist, but I believe that he should also be given equal credit for being a dreamer.

"It was his dream that brought us to the moon."

The life of Dr. Wernher von Braun reminds us that every good thing is the result of a dreamer dreaming great dreams, and then getting down to work. Thoreau remarked: "If you have built castles in the air, your work need not be lost; that is where they should be. Now put the foundations under them."

It takes creative imagination to produce something worth having. It takes creative imagination to be something. You must possess a mental grasp of the thing, conceive a desire to obtain it, and follow up the long process of development. The imagination always leads the way with a bright picture of the dream.

In the full-grown splendor of a *Saturn 5* rocket leaping up from its launching pad, people are too dazzled to remember the slow, preliminary work that went on for months in advance. Perhaps that is why the poet sings:

> In the hush of the Valley of Silence,
>   I dream all the songs that I sing;
> And the music floats down the dim Valley,
>   Till each finds a word for a wing,
> That to men, like the Dove of the Deluge,
>   A message of Peace they may bring.

Dr. Wernher von Braun is not alone in demonstrating the power of a dream. Abraham Lincoln would never have sat down before a polished table in the White House to liberate a people unless he had yearned in eager silence for this opportunity of a lifetime. Pasteur would not have given the world vaccination unless he first had dreamed of a conquest over germs.

A young, dreamy boy was reading Kane's *Arctic Explorations*. Suddenly he found himself fascinated by the wild, untamed North. The magnetic attraction grew and became a dream which, after twenty-three years of struggle, defeat, and trial, still glowed in his imagination and urged him on. His name became a household word for courage, endurance, unbreakable will, and iron determination. The result: Robert E. Peary invaded the frozen stretches of snow and ice that barred the way to the North Pole. The great explorer captured the prize for which, for nearly four hundred years, men had striven and died.

In 1854 a young man with a dream came to Kansas to start a town of his own. He called it "To-pe-ka," which is Indian for "Good Place to Dig Potatoes." People laughed at the young dreamer, but seven years later Cyrus K. Holliday had the thrill of seeing his "Good Place to Dig Potatoes" become the capital of the Kansas Territory.

Holliday now dreamed new dreams set to the rhythm of steam and steel. He dreamed of a train with a great destiny; a train that would cut across the prairie from the Missouri River to Colorado, stab the lofty mountains of the West, and come to rest at the salt waters of the Pacific.

Again people laughed. But three years later men came swinging heavy sledges and driving spikes. To the clanging thunder of a great anvil chorus, the tracks leaped across the prairie. Mileposts sprang up like magic. Town after town was left behind — Hutchinson, Great Bend, Dodge City, Pueblo, the Raton Pass. The dream came true, and the Santa Fe ranked among the great railroads of the world. Holliday's Santa Fe was a dream in steel come to life.

Father Jacques Marquette dreamed of following the

sunset to the shores of a great river which Illinois Indians said rolled "far to the west."

On June 17, 1673, Father Marquette's dream came true. A light canoe bearing Father Marquette shot out from the swift waters of the Wisconsin River into the broad expanse of the Mississippi. The sight of the mighty Mississippi made the party of explorers pause in thrilled silence. The height of the bluffs and the grandeur of the great river so awed the men that all Father Marquette could write in his journal for that day was: "With joy that we could not express, we entered the Mississippi."

That night the tired party of explorers beached their canoes at the foot of the great bluff overlooking the river, and Father Marquette gave the Mississippi a new name — the River of the Immaculate Conception.

Little did Father Marquette realize that the spot on which he was standing was to become Wyalusing State Park and that his exploits of that June 17 would be commemorated there with a beautiful plaque. Nor did Father Marquette dream that a picturesque little town on the Iowa side of the river would be named after him and that the State of Wisconsin would perpetuate his memory by placing a marble statue of him in Statuary Hall, Washington, D.C.

The power of a dream is as mighty as the spirit of man itself. Look across America today. St. Paul, St. Louis, Santa Fe, Los Angeles, and a litany of other cities are dreams of missionaries — dreams that once quickened the pulse of early European missionaries intent on establishing the kingdom of God in the New World. The missionary can apply to himself these words from Arthur W.E. O'Shaughnessy's "Ode":

We are the music-makers,
And we are the dreamers of dreams,
Wandering by lone sea-breakers,
And sitting by desolate streams;

140

World-losers and world-forsakers,
On whom the pale moon gleams:
Yet we are the movers and shakers
Of the world for ever, it seems.

A number of summers ago, when I was in the Black Hills of South Dakota, I was thrilled to receive an invitation to have dinner with the famous artist Lincoln Borglum. During the meal in his beautiful forest home, Lincoln mentioned to me how his father, Gutzon, dreamed of turning an acre and a half of vertical mountain into four faces. Lincoln worked side by side with his father on Mount Rushmore, then completed the work when Gutzon died. Today the faces of Washington, Jefferson, Roosevelt, and Lincoln look out in noble dignity from the granite heights of Mount Rushmore in the Black Hills of South Dakota. The stone faces represent a dream captured in stone.

The German poet Goethe described imagination as man's most important faculty. To this Albert Einstein agreed, adding that "imagination is more important than knowledge."

Alan Lovelace, acting director of NASA, depicts Dr. Wernher von Braun as "a twentieth-century Columbus who pushed back the new frontiers of outer space with efforts that enabled his adopted country to achieve preeminence in space exploration."

Von Braun's fellow worker, Ernst Stuhlinger, considered him an excellent engineer with an almost uncanny ability to visualize both a problem and its solution.

It is to the praise and glory of von Braun that he ignored both the criticism and the praise heaped upon him and, instead, concentrated on his second dream — his goal of turning the space age into a time for international cooperation.

"I look forward to the day," von Braun said, "when mankind will join hands to apply the combined technological ingenuity of all nations to the exploration and utilization of outer space for peaceful uses." This second dream has not yet come true, but von Braun's work has certainly helped to bring it closer.

Astronaut James McDivitt gave me still another insight into the character of Dr. Wernher von Braun. He was a man of confidence. When von Braun was once asked what it would take to build a rocket to reach the moon, he replied simply: "the will to do it."

The life of von Braun reminds us that human life is a poetic task: to use our imagination to invent the character we dream of being and should be. "In this sense," says Felix Marti-Ibanez, "human life is a kind of literature, a pure novel created by our fantasy, and our career is the Nobel prize awarded to that fantasy."

In the notes which he sent to me, von Braun remarked that "Man's most precious resource undoubtedly is his brain." The more I learn about Dr. Wernher von Braun, the more I'm impressed by two things — the tremendous sweep of his intellect, and his religious optimism. Von Braun was interested in everything from the far reaches of space to the history of the American West.

Among my greatest treasures are the personal notes which Dr. Wernher von Braun gave me prior to his death. In them, he strikes a note of high religious optimism.

"When man, almost two thousand years ago," von Braun wrote, "was given the opportunity to know Jesus Christ, to know God, who had decided to live for a while as man amongst fellowmen on this little planet, our world was turned upside down through the widespread witness of those who heard and understood Him."

That same miracle, says von Braun, can happen again if only all men will accept Christ. "I am also confident," continues von Braun, "that as we learn more and more about nature, we shall not only arrive at universally accepted scientific findings, but also at a universally accepted set of ethical standards for human behavior.

"This may sound like a highly optimistic statement in view of all the atrocities and acts of terror committed in our time. Alright, so maybe I am an optimist. I am convinced that in spite of all temporary setbacks there is a slow but steady upward trend in mankind's universal standard of ethics.

"Take the case of slavery. In antiquity, slavery was considered a perfectly normal thing. For the Greek and Roman civilizations it was an essential element in their way of life. The idea of developing a civilization without some people having to do the dirty work so others could write their poetry was considered absurd. Even during the early nineteenth century the thought of operating a cotton plantation in the southern United States without slaves was considered impractical. Yet today the very concept of slavery is universally condemned and labeled as repulsive, even in totalitarian countries.

"Science and technology undoubtedly made decisive contributions to the abolishment of slavery. They have provided everyone with a wide assortment of electrically and gasoline-powered slaves which once and for all did away with the need for any human slaves.

"I am certain that this, too, was a part of the master plan of our Maker. In the world around us we can behold the obvious manifestations of His divine plan wherever we look. We behold the gift of love. And we are humbled by the powerful forces at work on a galactic scale, and the purposeful orderliness of nature that endows a tiny and ungainly seed with the ability to develop into a beautiful flower.

"Although I know of no reference to Christ ever commenting on scientific work, I do know that He said: 'Ye shall know the truth and the truth shall make you free.' Thus, I am certain that were He among us today, Christ would encourage scientific research as modern man's most noble striving to comprehend and admire His Father's handiwork.

"In this reaching of the new millennium through faith in the words of Jesus Christ, science can be a valuable tool rather than an impediment. The universe as revealed through scientific inquiry is the living witness that God has indeed been at work. Understanding the nature of the creation provides a basis for the faith by which we attempt to know the nature of the Creator."

Faith and prayer were interwoven into the fabric of Dr. Wernher von Braun's life. And this same spirit that animated von Braun ran throughout the entire Apollo project like a thread of pure gold in a tapestry.

99

DEMCO